Doul

Blessing

Double

Blessing

Our Journey Through

Adoption

Pip John

Published by CompletelyNovel.com 2014

First published in Great Britain in 2014 by CompletelyNovel.com

ISBN 9781849144612

Acknowledgements

I want to thank my amazing family and friends who have been a massive support to Stacey and I. They have been on this journey with us all the way; we are so blessed to have them in our lives.

Thanks to my Mum, my boss Anna and my friend Eve for proof reading and giving me your suggestions.

Thanks to my wonderful husband Stacey for putting up with me while writing this book. You are my rock and I couldn't have done any of it without you.

Thank you God for bringing two wonderful children into our lives and making our family complete.

For my forever family, I love you, always.

Introduction

As I sit here and write this introduction, I still can't believe I have achieved this. I never thought I would write a book. I love books and love reading but it never crossed my mind to write one of my own. I was asked by our adoption agency to write an article about my adoption experience; something for the newsletter. It took me long enough to come up with an idea for what to write and that was just a small article! When I finally did write the piece I had a lot of positive feedback from my friends.

It was my dad who first suggested I write a book about our experience. I mentioned it to my husband Stacey, who also thought it was a good idea. At first I was adamant, no way; I'm not a writer, where would I start? Would anyone be interested in what I had to say? But the thought wouldn't leave. I began to think about how I would structure the book and the little anecdotal stories I could include. I started to feel the excitement grow, and I felt that maybe I could give it a go.

So here it is; my book. Although it has taken a while to complete, it was actually a pleasure to write in the end. Remembering everything we have gone through together, the ups, and the downs. It has been an adventure, one which at times felt overwhelming but also exceeded all our hopes and expectations. I have read books while going through this process from various experts and organisations, literature about adoption and what to expect. I guess the aim of my book is not to be an information book about how to adopt, or what to expect when adopting. It's more about my personal journey through infertility and the adoption process, how I felt going through it; the good points, and the low points. It's just an honest account of every step of the process, the way

I saw it. If anyone out there is thinking about adopting or

is going through adoption at the moment, this book may

help them to get a feel for what they are about to embark

on. Adoption is a lengthy, personal and emotional

experience, everyone is different, every child is different,

and every situation is different. This is my story, I hope

you enjoy reading it, and maybe there will parts in here

that you will relate to, maybe there will be parts in here

that didn't affect you the way it did me. Most of all I want

this book to be an uplifting read, to see beyond the hard

times, the frustration, and the pain and to celebrate in the

rewards that adoption brings; the children that burst into

your life and completely and utterly sweep you off your

feet and melt your heart. I hope it inspires and motivates

those who are on the brink to just go for it, because it is so

worth it, I promise.

Chapter One

Infertility

I was 25 when I got married; I was one of those girls who had always dreamed of getting married. Ever since I was a teenager I was excited at the prospect of being married and sharing my life with someone. I knew that was what I wanted. I was on the right path with my career. I had achieved my science degree, had a job that I really enjoyed and was progressing nicely up the ladder. I was never hugely ambitious when it came to my career. I wanted a job where I could help people and make a difference, but I didn't have to be some high flying executive or anything. As long as I knew I was progressing the right way, I was happy.

So when I met Stacey, I felt I was ready to get married. I wanted to take the next step. Fortunately for me, Stacey wanted the same thing.

As I stood in front of Stacey on our wedding day, and we said our vows, little did I know that we had a steam train hurtling towards us threatening to knock us down. That steam train was called infertility. Infertility was not something I had ever thought about in any detail. I didn't know anyone that had gone through it. That steam train has knocked us over a couple of times along our journey but, because of our strong marriage and faith, we were able to get back up and keep on going.

I remember when we had our first conversation about starting a family. We had been married about a year, I had been on the pill and then one day I forgot to take it. I told Stacey there may be a chance I was pregnant. (If only

I had known!) We weren't ready at that stage. We were still quite young and wanted to experience more together before starting a family. We had thought it would be about two years before contemplating starting a family. So it was a strange few weeks for me as we waited to find out if I was pregnant or not. I had mixed feelings, a bit worried – we weren't ready, how would we manage? It was too soon. However after it sunk in, I started to feel excited at the prospect of having a baby.

In the end, it was a false alarm and I wasn't pregnant. However it had started a train of thought that made me realise that actually I didn't mind starting our family sooner than we had planned. We talked about it and decided we would give it a few more months and then stop the pill permanently and see what happened.

Chapter Two

IVF

After a year of trying (and failing) to fall pregnant, I decided to have some tests. I had been told by so many people that it could take a long time, it didn't always happen straight away, so I wasn't overly worried at this stage. I visited the GP and explained our situation and she conducted some tests and checked me over. Everything came back okay; I was then prescribed a few months of a fertility drug called clomid which was unsuccessful, so she referred me to the hospital for further tests.

By the time I had my appointment at the hospital I had started to feel a bit more apprehensive. I started to wonder why this wasn't happening for us. There must be something wrong. Stacey and I started to feel a bit bogged down with the effort of it all; having to have sex on certain days of the month, charting my temperature so I would know when I was ovulating. It became so clinical and not romantic at all. What was supposed to have been special turned out to be anything but. It felt like it had become a military operation. It was a really tough time for both of us. It was difficult, frustrating and hard going. It wasn't how we envisioned our lives would be. There were times of strain between myself and Stacey and we had to work through those times.

Undertaking fertility testing is not the nicest experience. It can be uncomfortable, undignified and just very unpleasant. However, I was keen to have the tests because I was hoping to get some answers and find out what was wrong. In the end, the tests we both had all came back normal. They put our difficulty conceiving down to unexplained infertility. In one way it was a relief to know there was nothing wrong, but in another way it was frustrating to know that they couldn't do anything to help us.

The hospital told us there was nothing further they could do and we discussed the option of IVF. It was a big decision, deciding to go for IVF. I had heard quite a lot about it by then. Mainly that it was a very low success rate, that it was very difficult; emotionally and physically. Stacey and I discussed it with each other and our close families. In the end we decided that we would like to try. I was so desperate to have a child that I couldn't think of the possibility of not going through it, however unlikely the chances were. We were in the fortunate position that we were able to get up to three cycles of IVF free on the NHS. The hospital referred us to a clinic in Cambridgeshire and our first cycle of IVF begun in 2008.

Once implantation is completed, the only thing left is the dreaded two week wait! (2WW). After the 2WW, a pregnancy test is taken to determine if the IVF has been successful.

For the first cycle I chose local anaesthetic and was given pethidine. The egg retrieval was successful (but quite painful) and they retrieved eight eggs. Those eggs were then fertilised with the sperm and left for five days to see if they survived to the blastocyst stage. I only had two embryos (blastocysts) left after the five days and so they were both implanted.

Even though the egg retrieval went well and eight eggs were successfully retrieved I had a really bad reaction to the pethidine. Usually within an hour or so of having egg retrieval (with local anaesthetic) you should be ready to go home, however on my first cycle I was at the clinic literally all day because I was so poorly. Each time I sat up, the blood drained from my face and I felt like I was going to pass out. I had to lie down the whole time. I went a funny grey colour and got all hot and sweaty. It was the strangest (not to mention most embarrassing) experience. I had to go on a drip to rehydrate myself, I couldn't eat anything. I was looked after so well by the lovely nurses but I think even they were wondering when I would be ready to go home. I was the first person to enter the ward that morning and as the day wore on I watched each of the other ladies leaving to go home until I was on my own.

After several failed attempts to sit up without nearly passing out, I finally started to feel a bit better so the nurses decided to try me with some sugar to get my energy up. I was given a mars bar, which I obediently ate. We then decided to try and walk to the toilet around the corner to see how I felt. As soon as I got to the toilet, the mars bar decided to make a re-appearance in the sink. As soon as I was sick, I started feeling better quite quickly. I could feel the colour returning to my face and just felt stronger. I finally felt able to walk without feeling like I was going to pass out. Not long after that, I felt ready to go home.

Waiting to see if any of my eight follicles had reached the blastocyst stage was quite nerve racking. As this was my first cycle, I was a bit naive to the uncertainties of it all. I didn't realise how risky it all was, how many steps there were that could go wrong. I just assumed it would all be fine, get them implanted and wait to see if it had worked! In truth, there are actually a lot of steps that could potentially go wrong,

The two week wait following implantation was probably the hardest part of it all. It felt like the longest two weeks of my life. I tried to keep busy to take my mind off it, but that was nearly impossible. Every little twinge in my body made me question what was happening. Is it a period pain? Or is it a sign of implantation? The trouble is the symptoms of implantation can be very similar to those you get before your period so it really was very difficult. It was constantly on my mind. However, eventually, the wait came to an end and I was ready to take the pregnancy test.

Chapter Four

Harsh Reality

It was positive! I couldn't believe it! I literally couldn't believe it. So many times in the past I had done this test with the result always being negative; I had never experienced a positive pregnancy test. It was one of those moments I had dreamt about for so long. I had done countless pregnancy tests just praying that one day one of them would be positive. Now here I was, sitting on the toilet after the two week wait of my first cycle of IVF staring incredulously at a positive pregnancy test. I couldn't put into words how happy I was in that moment. Just before taking the test, I was shaking because I was so nervous not daring to hope but absolutely desperate to find out. It was the most amazing feeling ever! I felt pure elation! All those hard years of trying for a baby and I was finally pregnant! I could actually say it, I was pregnant! How I had longed to be able to say those words!

I hadn't slept a wink the night before; all I could think about was the pregnancy test I was going to take in the morning. I tossed and turned, desperate for the morning to arrive. I was so nervous; it all hinged on this result. I was trying to keep my excitement in check because I didn't know the result and I wanted to be careful just in case it was negative. In my heart however, I had this conviction that it had worked and I just couldn't wait to get out of bed that morning to do the test.

I had left Stacey in bed snoring away. (How could he sleep? – Didn't he know what a momentous day this was going to be?) I did the test with trembling hands.

As soon as I had the result, I ran into the bedroom, woke up Stacey and told him. His reaction was a lot less exuberant than mine but that's just his way, I knew he was as happy as I was. Finally we were going to have a baby. It was all we both wanted, what we had been longing for, for so long and now finally it had happened. We had seen so many of our friends fall pregnant and now it was our turn.

I texted my friend Claire in Australia and told her because she was one of the few people who knew we were going through it. I was desperate to see and tell my mum but I had to wait for the right moment to tell her as she had no idea we were doing this. I couldn't wait to tell her! Stacey and I sat up in bed chatting away (well I did most of the chatting) about it, we were just over the moon; it still hadn't quite sunk in. I didn't know what all the fuss was about with IVF, people telling me how hard it was; I thought it had been fairly straight forward really. I wasn't particularly hormonal or stressed out. Yes, the wait was difficult, but apart from that, it was fine. I couldn't stop smiling the whole day; it was the most amazing feeling. We didn't tell anyone that day (which was so difficult because I wanted to shout it from the rooftops). I had told my friends at work that the test was a couple of days later because I just wanted to have a couple of days in case it was negative to feel a bit stronger before telling them. As it happened I didn't need those few days.

I rang up the clinic to tell them our good news. They were very happy for me and just asked to do another test in a week's time and then ring them again with the result. If it was still positive they would book me in for a scan.

We had planned to tell my family over a meal out, somewhere nice but actually in reality, I just couldn't wait that long to tell them. I knew how happy they would be for us because they knew how much we wanted this. It would be such wonderful news for the family, something exciting to be happening. A couple of nights later we went over my parents' house. We had it all planned how we were going to tell them but I was so excited that as soon as I got there and sat down I just blurted it out "I'm pregnant!" I couldn't help myself; this was something I had been desperate to talk about to them, especially my mum, for so long, that I couldn't hold it in any longer.

Their faces when I told them were a picture, they were stunned! It was so funny. They couldn't believe we had gone through the whole IVF process. Even though they knew we were considering it and looking at it, they had no idea. It was such a great and emotional night. Everyone was so happy for us and we were all so excited. Stacey's parents live in Birmingham and even though we would have loved to tell them to their faces, we knew we had to tell them straight away, so we called them to tell them. They were so happy for us. Those few days after finding out were so wonderful. I can't express the depth of my happiness. Even though it was early days, I was wondering about when the baby would be born (July), would it be a little boy or girl? Stacey and I went out for dinner one evening that week and spent the whole evening talking about it and the future, it was fantastic.

The following week I did another pregnancy test and it was still positive, so I rang the clinic again and we booked a date for a couple of weeks later to have our first scan.

The next week went by in a whirl. I was thinking about being pregnant pretty much all the time and had this wonderful feeling of contentment, the future looked bright. At last I was going to be a mummy!

It was the following Wednesday while I was at work when my world came crashing down. It had been just over three weeks since our first positive pregnancy test and I was still feeling amazing and looking forward the scan which was booked for the following Monday.

I was sitting with my patient at work carrying out a hearing test when I felt a stabbing pain in my lower stomach. Suddenly a cold fear gripped me. I knew what that feeling was. Period pain; it was all too familiar to me. I somehow managed to get through the appointment with my patient and as soon as he left, I went to the toilet. It confirmed my worst fear. It felt like someone was squeezing my heart so tight, I couldn't breathe. I was shaking. I thought I was going to be sick. People who have gone through IVF will know exactly the feelings I was going through. This couldn't be happening. I had to pull myself together because I was at work, I had to try and get through the rest of the day. I went back to my office and just tried to calm myself down enough to get through my last patient of the day. The pain had stopped so I somehow managed to get through it. As soon as I could, I left work, I didn't say anything to anyone just walked out and drove home. I was in shock, I couldn't believe that in an instant my dream had crumbled and it was over. When I pulled the car over at my house I called Stacey and all I told him was that I needed him.

He came home straight away and as soon as I saw him, I just broke down. I couldn't keep it in anymore, I felt devastated, I couldn't believe it was over, I wasn't pregnant anymore, I had suffered an early miscarriage. I told Stacey and he was great. He just helped me and reassured me we would get through it together. The pain I felt was indescribable. Not only was I sad for me and my loss, but I felt like I had let Stacey down, that my stupid body was broken and couldn't do anything right. I cried for the lost future I had dreamed about, I cried for the baby that we would no longer have. It was the worst feelings I have ever been through in my life. It was so raw. My heart was broken. It was then that I realised how difficult IVF really was. I had flippantly thought how easy and straightforward it was but when the realisation hit me that we would have to go through it all again, it felt like the end of the world. It's such a long and emotional process with no guarantees at the end.

I went into the first cycle of IVF quite naively, thinking that it would all be fine, I was aware that miscarriages could happen but I didn't think it would happen to me. Now here I was faced with this very grim reality that yes it could and we were back to the start again. It was so awful. I just couldn't stop crying. I got into bed and didn't get out for about two days, just cried and cried. The only reason I got through it was because I had Stacey and my family. Stacey was my rock, he was there lying next to me on the bed holding me until I started to feel better. He was obviously in a lot of pain too but he was only thinking of me. It was a very low time for us both.

Chapter Five

IVF Cycle Two

The word I would use to describe my feelings during the
second IVF cycle would be stressful. After the
disappointment of the last cycle, I was much more aware
of the uncertainties and risks associated with IVF. I felt so
much more was riding on this. We were so desperate for a
child, the thought of it being unsuccessful and having to go
through it again made me feel very anxious. I was aware
that we only had a couple more chances of trying IVF. I
was more nervous at each stage; would I have another bad
experience at retrieval? Did I have enough follicles?
Would they survive to blastocyst stage? Every step felt like
a massive ordeal for me. I tried to relax but I just kept
remembering what had happened on the last cycle. I kept

thinking that even if I had another positive result how long before I could relax and accept that I was pregnant?

The retrieval was much better this time. I didn't have pethidine and I was absolutely fine after the procedure, although it was more painful because no anaesthetic. Everything went well, I had a good number of follicles, two of which survived until the blastocyst stage and were implanted successfully.

The two week wait was very difficult. I was stressed the whole time. The other thing that happened during the 2WW was the dreaded shoulder pain.

For years I have suffered with this shoulder pain. I remember when it first happened. I woke up one morning in complete agony, and I thought I had broken my shoulder. I had severe pains in my right shoulder which went to my chest making it painful to breathe. I couldn't move my arm. I had to take a day off work because I was in so much pain. Over the following few days the pain eased off. I had no idea what it was and over the next few months, every so often this pain would come back. I thought maybe I had pulled a muscle in my chest. I went to the GP about it and they said I might have a weak muscle in my chest and every so often I would do something which pulls the muscle. The shoulder pain could be a referred pain.

This went on for a while until I realised these shoulder/chest pains happened every time I had a period. I would get a pain in my shoulder and then the next day my period would start. It was almost like a signal or sign that my period was on its way. I didn't think too much of it to start with, just thought of it as a period pain. People often get strange pains sometimes; it's just part of life. I started thinking more about it as we started looking into fertility testing and IVF. I wondered if there was a link to why I couldn't fall pregnant.

I started researching the internet and found out about diaphragmatic endometriosis.

Diaphragmatic endometriosis is a rare form of the condition, and one of its main symptoms is shoulder pain. All the symptoms I read about were exactly the same as the symptoms I had. I couldn't believe how many different types of endometriosis there were. I happened to have one of the rarest and difficult to treat. I looked into whether this type of endometriosis could affect fertility. The diaphragm is not associated with reproduction so I was quite confused by it. I couldn't really get any conclusive answers.

As I was going through the two week wait on my second cycle, I had the shoulder pain so I immediately thought, that's it then; the IVF hasn't worked. I couldn't remember having the shoulder pain during the first cycle of IVF. I was so stressed during that two week wait, it felt like the longest two weeks of my life. I kept crying every so often because I knew it hadn't worked. I just wanted to get it over and done with so we could move on again. Stacey said I was just being negative and that I shouldn't assume anything until we knew for sure. However I knew my body and I knew what the shoulder pain meant. I had experienced it for many years and I knew my period was coming. Everything felt different this cycle, I just knew in my heart of hearts it wasn't going to happen.

As it turned out my doubts were proved to be correct. I did the pregnancy test as required after my two week wait and sure enough it was negative; I wasn't pregnant. I was very upset, had a cry but this time I was more prepared for the disappointment. I kind of knew all along this wasn't going to work. I felt really sad that this was happening, I felt sad that I couldn't conceive children on my own, that we had to go through IVF. It was so difficult to keep going, but I couldn't bear the thought of not having children.

I decided to ask the consultant about this shoulder pain. I had researched about endometriosis in general and realised I hadn't had the procedure they perform when diagnosing endometriosis. I thought that if I did have this endometriosis of the diaphragm, perhaps I had patches in other places and maybe that was the cause of my infertility. I also thought that if they did find endometriosis, could they treat it and would that help our chances? I was actually surprised that I hadn't had the procedure (laparoscopy) for diagnosing endometriosis already. If I could have this laparoscopy then maybe there was something they could do to help me. I was quite fired up, filled with a new hope that maybe I would get some answers. So far all they had said was unexplained infertility. I had diagnosed this myself, so I needed to be sure I was on the right track.

I went back to my GP and asked to be re-referred to the hospital for a laparoscopy. The GP was happy to do that for me and before long I had an appointment with a Consultant Gynaecologist. She agreed straight away to the laparoscopy (which made me wonder why they didn't do this at the start).

The result of the laparoscopy was that I did have endometriosis of the uterus and the patches they found were cauterised. The Consultant said she couldn't see any endometriosis on the diaphragm. To make things a bit more complicated, the diaphragm wasn't her area of expertise so if there were any patches on the diaphragm I would need a thoracic surgeon to do the operation. The

Consultant felt that after this laparoscopy, our fertility

should be improved, she was hopeful that things would be

better for us.

I was so pleased to hear that, finally to have some positive

news. I felt very happy about the result of the laparoscopy.

I just wished I had pushed for it sooner.

However, after a few more months I still hadn't fallen

pregnant, so we went through for our next cycle of IVF.

Before the laparoscopy we had been referred for our third

cycle of IVF. I felt more positive this time about it all. I

knew that it may not happen but I was determined for it

not to take over my life. I wanted to remain positive until

I knew otherwise. I did my best to keep busy and take my

mind off all the waiting. This time I ended up having

general anaesthetic because they weren't keen on doing it

without any kind of anaesthetic. I told them I had nothing

last time (except gas and air) and I was fine but they still weren't sure. They explained that they had an anaesthetist in the ward because one of the other ladies was having general, and if I changed my mind, they could sedate me too. I wasn't sure about having general so I said I would leave it. However when they started the procedure, it turned out to be quite painful and they said there were a lot of follicles to retrieve. In the end we decided the best option was for me to have the general anaesthetic. It went so well, I wished I'd had it every time. I was asleep throughout and when I woke, felt absolutely fine. They took twenty follicles out which is the most I had produced so was a very good result. I remained hopeful through the 2WW that maybe this would be the time it would work.

It was negative. I put my head in my hands and waited for those all too familiar feelings to hit me. I don't know why I was so shocked again, it was my third time trying, I should have expected it. The thing was nothing can prepare you for the feelings you experience when your whole life has been set around this two minute test that you have been waiting for the last painstakingly slow two weeks to do. This being our third time going through IVF didn't make it any easier to deal with. Here I was, sitting on the toilet looking at the pregnancy test which was telling me, yet again, I was not pregnant. My heart started to race and I had that panicky feeling that I was going to pass out. I felt the blood drain from my face and I just felt despair, I was disappointed and frustrated. Above all I felt incredibly sad. As the tears started to fall, all I could think was I had failed again. My body had failed me and there was nothing I could do about it. It just seemed so unfair. I felt like I had let my husband down yet again. How could it be so hard to fall pregnant? All my friends were getting pregnant, how come it wasn't working for me? Here I was again, third failed IVF, this time a different emotion started bubbling up inside me something I hadn't really felt before - anger. I felt like I had done everything I possibly could, I'd had years of trying naturally, I'd had test after test; I'd had three cycles of IVF, a heart breaking miscarriage. I'd had all my friends and family praying and supporting us. The anger and frustration was overwhelming, I felt so let down. What more could I do? How much more could I give? The answer to that question ended being no more, that was it, I couldn't go through it again; I was done.

I was desperate to speak to Stacey; he was the only one who knew what I was going through. Throughout all of this process he had been my rock, the one with whom I could completely be myself. I didn't have to put a brave face on things or try to be positive when inside I was scared or worried. He has always been there for me one hundred per cent. When times have been tough, I have clung to him both figuratively and literally. Going through infertility as a couple isn't easy. There have been times where the strain has shown, but we have got through it by communicating and being there for each other. We were in it together.

A few weeks went by and we slowly got back to normal, trying to put the disappointment behind us. The anger lasted a couple of days and then after a lot of praying, I found comfort in God, and knew all I could do was trust him that he was in control and he wanted what was best for me. I perhaps didn't know what that was at the time, but that's where my faith stepped in. Once I had acknowledged that, I began to feel a lot more positive about the future. I felt that we had come to the end of the road as far as IVF was concerned. Going through IVF is a gruelling process. There are many difficult steps along the way. As soon as you get through one uncertainty, another one comes along. It really tests you mentally. As soon as you start to feel positive, the next challenge arrives. It is physically demanding also. The amount of drug and hormone injections, suppositories, blood tests, internal scans you have to endure, really takes its toll on your body. It is a daily battle to choose to remain positive and not to sink down and fear the worst. You have to prepare yourself for the worst while hoping for the best. It's a tough balancing act.

That was why after our third unsuccessful IVF procedure, I made the decision not to try anymore. It was too much; the thought of starting all over again just filled me with dread. I just couldn't do it anymore. The thought of going back to the clinic, made me want to cry. (Not to mention the cost!). The only thing was, I hadn't told Stacey how I felt. Both of us had to make this decision; his opinion was very important to me so we needed to discuss it. It was almost as if we had been putting it off, neither of us saying much about it. One evening I decided to broach the elephant in the room and tentatively asked Stacey how he was feeling about our situation and the future. I was careful not to tell him my thoughts until I had heard where he was at. To my relief, Stacey was feeling exactly the same as me; he didn't want to go through anymore IVF either. (Or more to the point he didn't want to watch me have to go through it all again). I think he felt reluctant to say it to me in case I wanted to carry on (and Stacey being Stacey would have gone along with whatever I wanted). We had made the decision- no more IVF; that was over with. It was like a weight had lifted off my shoulders. I had mixed feelings. Sadness at the fact that it meant I probably would never have my own children naturally, and as a woman, that is a difficult thing to come to terms with, but immense relief that the pressure was off. I wouldn't have to go through it again. I decided to broach a new subject, one that we had mentioned before briefly when we originally discussed our options.

"Stace, what do you think about looking into adopting?" I looked at him expectantly. He smiled.

"Yes let's look into adoption".

I smiled back feeling the excitement building inside.

The next chapter on our journey was about to begin - Adoption.

Chapter Six

May 2011

The Phone Call

I found a nice bench to sit on in the outdoor area of the hospital where I work. This alone was a near miracle; to find an empty bench when the weather was so nice was very unlikely. Usually they were all taken by the time I got to have my lunch break. I put down all my paraphernalia on the bench, all the scribbled notes, all the different websites I had found and all the phone numbers. I had been researching all about who to contact about adopting, which agency to go with and which numbers to call for further information.

So, armed with this information I prepared to make a phone call to our local agency to ask about the possibility of adopting. In my head, I had it all planned out what I wanted. People had told me different things about adopting. Their experiences or people they had known who had adopted, but I was very naive coming into this process. I expected to give them a call, tell them what we were hoping to do and what kind of expectations we had, and they would explain how that would all work. I was hopeful that we would be accepted because we were a fairly young married couple in our mid-thirties. We had a three bedroom house; we were quite experienced youth workers. We also had reasonably paid jobs. I thought this should be fairly easy.

Stacey and I had discussed our desires about who we wanted to adopt. We wanted to adopt a baby, didn't mind the sex, and didn't mind the race. Stacey is of Caribbean

39

descent and I am Caucasian, so we thought it would be nice to adopt a mixed race child. We would adopt one baby only at this stage and if everything went well we would look into adopting more. Well I think you can guess it isn't quite as straightforward as that. I didn't really have a clue about adopting and what it involved, but I was about to be enlightened.

"Well Mrs John, let me just give you some information just to set your expectations at the right level."

"Firstly, you can't adopt a baby; the youngest you can adopt are children one years old and over."

Bang, first arrow of disappointment.

"You would have to go through an information evening and an interview to see if you are allowed to go onto the adoption course."

Second arrow. I felt my heart sink; wow it was going to be harder than I thought.

"There are very few mixed race children available to adopt, so you may have to wait a long time."

This information was surprising to me, but I could accept it because we weren't so fixed on the race.

"You would then have to go through an adoption course, a home study course with your social worker, an approval panel, a matching panel and if all that goes to plan, introductions before placement."

By now I was feeling extremely overwhelmed with enormity of the situation and the sheer amount of information I had just been given. What did it all mean? It was so much to take on board; I was very disappointed that we wouldn't be able to adopt a baby. I thought that we would be able to, so Stacey and I would be able to experience being parents to a baby. At the end of the call, I asked for an information pack to be sent so we could have a look through and read about the process in more detail.

I hung up feeling quite overwhelmed and disappointed. With a heavy heart I went back to my office wondering if we could do this. Would we go through all those stages and not even adopt a baby? How old would the child be? If we wanted to do this we had to be sure, we had to be serious that this was right for us. We couldn't enter into this lightly; it was a big decision, and one which needed much thought. The doubts started to creep in. How I got through that day at work without talking to Stacey, I'll never know. I was itching to tell him everything but I had to wait until I got home.

Chapter Seven

June 2011

The Information Evening

As a person, I can be very indecisive. I find it hard to make decisions. Even decisions like what film to watch at the cinema is a big issue for me, especially if we are in a group. I would much rather other people make the decision than me, I don't like the responsibility. Sometimes when I do make decisions, I am easily swayed out of them by someone else's view point. I wish I could be more single minded and have the courage of my convictions but I let doubts creep in and often start to question if this is really the right thing.

It was particularly important in our journey through adoption for me to be sure that it was definitely what I wanted. I had to know for certain that was right for me. I couldn't be indecisive about this. After the phone call, I was left feeling quite dejected and unsure. I was so optimistic and excited about it before hand and thought I had it all sussed out and then with one conversation, all the doubts started flooding in. Was this really the right path for us? Stacey is quite a sanguine kind of personality so he is laid back about everything. When I mentioned to him my doubts or how overwhelmed I was feeling, he just said, "don't worry, we have plenty of time to decide. Just take it a day at a time and we'll see how we feel." What I really wanted him to say was, "we are doing the right thing, I know you are feeing nervous about it, but we can do it." That would have given me the confidence I needed to know that it was the right thing to do. In hindsight however, I realised that I had to make my own decision. Going through the adoption process, I had to be one hundred per cent sure we were doing the right thing. Any doubts and we would have struggled to get through it. If you are sure of what you are doing, even when the hard times come, you are committed to the process and you know in your heart it is the right thing to do, it will make it so much easier. I also realised that I was going to be the driving force in this journey. Stacey was going to be my rock through it all, and my support, but it was me that was going to be pushing it through. I needed to be sure.

We read through the information pack that came through following the phone call. It pretty much said the same sort of thing that I was told on the phone. It asked us to fill in a form if we wanted to attend an information evening.

We decided we would go to the next information evening because it would give us some more information about the adoption process and we would perhaps have a clearer picture in our head about what was involved.

On the evening of the meeting, I felt apprehensive. I was anxious to hear everything they had to say, I wanted to have clarity in a few areas. I still had nerves and doubts about adopting but was really hopeful that the meeting would allay those fears and put the doubts to bed. I needed confirmation that this was the right thing for us.

When we arrived, we sat down and had a quick look around. There were quite a lot of people there. I couldn't help but wonder what all their stories were; had they already got children; were they, like us, unable to conceive naturally? I am quite fascinated with people and love to people watch when I'm out and about, so my natural curiosity was aroused.

The information evening, was very informative (as you would expect) and it went through all aspects of the process; timings, appointments, meetings, panels etc. All this seemed okay because I had already been told this.

It was when they started to talk about the kind of children that needed adopting that my feelings started to change. They told us that children who needed adopting were often from abused and/or neglected backgrounds and may have challenging behaviours as a result. They may have issues with rejection and low self-esteem; they may have disabilities and there may be uncertainties about their development. One quote that stayed with me that night was that 'every child deserves a loving family.'

It broke my heart, that's how I would describe the evening. Even though they were telling us some very disturbing information, all I could think was, I have to do this. Instead of looking at things through my eyes as a prospective adopter, I suddenly saw it through the child's eyes. What the children needed, not what we needed; I felt a bit guilty for my selfish desires and wants, when all the time there were these beautiful children needing loving homes. I just wanted to adopt them all! It was a very enlightening and emotional evening.

I came out of the meeting knowing I wanted to adopt. Yes I still felt overwhelmed and anxious about the challenges ahead, but I had to do it, there was no way back now. I said as much to Stacey in the car and he wasn't quite as convinced as I was. I think because I had had the phone call and had already started processing a lot of the information they had told me, I was more ready to go for it. Stacey came out of that meeting feeling a bit like I felt after the phone call. He needed more time to process it all.

The one thing that is drummed into you, we were to learn, throughout the process is the worst case scenarios. The most challenging behaviours, the difficulties that lay ahead and the problems the children have attaching (or not) to their adoptive parents because of their previous experiences. Also the fact that babies below the age of one are very unlikely to be adopted is mentioned frequently throughout the process. I think that a lot of people going through the adoption process are hoping (like we were) to adopt a baby. I guess they feel they have to tell you the worst case scenarios to prepare you for what may lay ahead. It is very demoralising to keep hearing it. I also believe they could talk more about the rewards that adoption brings, because there are many rewards which far outweigh the negatives. I don't feel that this was really spoken about very much. The only times we heard the positives about adoption was from people who had already adopted themselves.

I was careful to give Stacey time to mull things over, aware that this was a big decision and that he needed space to work out what he thought about it all. However, because I felt so sure now, I was itching to get started and take the next step. I was so relieved that I had this strong desire to adopt; I needed to feel like that because as I said before, I can often be swayed by other people or challenges and doubts can enter my head. I now had that conviction deep down that this was right for us, I really did. It was this conviction that helped me through the difficult times that were ahead (and there were to be quite a few of those).

We had a conversation about it at home. I asked Stacey how he felt and whether I could go ahead and take the next step, which was an interview with a Social Worker. They would then decide if we were suitable to actually go onto the adoption process. He was quite surprised I asked him because he thought we had already decided to progress to the next stage. I was relieved that he was happy to move forward and so I fixed up a date to have our

interview.

Chapter Eight

July 2011

Counselling Interview

After our information evening, we were advised to contact the adoption and fostering team to schedule the next step which was the counselling interview. This involved meeting up with two Social Workers to discuss the adoption in more detail and our suitability to start the process.

I thought that meant a chat/discussion that wouldn't last long, about who we are, where we live, our jobs etc. They would then tell us a bit more about the adoption process and we would then decide if we wanted to go ahead with the adoption. How wrong was I? (There's a pattern emerging here).

I was keen to get started, now that I had a strong resolve that this was definitely what I wanted to do, I was eager to move things on.

The only way I could describe the counselling interview was like an intense job interview; I felt very much under scrutiny. They asked some very tricky questions which I wasn't expecting, about our views on adoption and what we thought it meant etc. I felt like we had to give them the most brilliant and profound answers so that they felt we were ready. They asked all about our past history with IVF and whether we felt we had moved on from that. Were we still grieving about not having children naturally? Had we come to terms with it all? A lot of the interview was centred on quite personal questions which I had not even considered. They asked all about our families, our jobs, our finances, our house, you name it they asked it! It was a very long interview; about an hour and a half, although it felt like a lot longer than that. It was just something that we couldn't really prepare for because we didn't know what we would be asked. Even though both Social Workers were pleasant (and one of them would end up being our own Social Worker, one with whom we got on very well with and supported us wholeheartedly), we didn't know them at that point and they didn't know us. As a result it felt quite tense and when we gave our answers a lot of the time they didn't give much away. Half the time I would be thinking, is that the right answer? Was that the right thing to say? It was quite exhausting to be honest.

Stacey and I have been youth leaders for many years. At the time of the adoption we were running youth clubs in the area where we lived, so they asked us quite a lot about all of that. Questions like how long we had being running the clubs? What ages were they aimed at? What behaviours had we encountered? What challenges had come our way? How we dealt with the challenging behaviours? I must admit, I was glad Stacey was there too, I have a lot of respect and admiration for people who adopt on their own. I imagine it is very hard going.

This was the second contact we had about adoption and again, as at the information evening, they talked a lot about the challenges of adopting. What we thought the challenges would be for us. They also discussed the kind of children who need adopting; children who had been abused and/or neglected and would possibly go on to exhibit challenging behaviours, how did we think we would cope with that?

A mention was also made relating to the fact that we wouldn't be able to adopt a baby younger than one year. One of the Social Workers commented that she had been working there five years and the youngest she had arranged adoption for was eleven months and that was very unusual. Yet again, the emphasis was on the negative or the worst case scenarios. I think they do that to make sure our expectations were at the right level so there would be no misunderstandings should we decide to pursue adoption. It was quite a heavy session, even though I was sure it is what I wanted to do, it was very demanding. I was still waiting for the feel good factor to kick in. Everything had just felt quite intense so far. I do understand why they have to do that, they are putting the needs of the children first and they need to make sure that prospective adopters know exactly what they are letting themselves in for by starting the adoption journey. They don't want people entering into it and then halfway along, deciding it isn't for them. You really do need to be one hundred per cent sure it is the right thing for you.

I must admit, even though they insist that it is very unlikely you will adopt a baby, I still had a feeling that for us it would be different. Maybe you could say I was in denial, I don't know, but all I do know was that I had this feeling and I wasn't going to give up hope that we would be able to adopt a baby.

The area I was slightly nervous about was telling them we were Christians. We had mentioned to several people that we were hoping to adopt and quite a few people gave us advice about not telling them we were Christians because it would go against us. They said not to be too open about it because it may harm our chances. It would have been very difficult not to mention it because it is such a massive part of our lives. We go to church regularly; we are youth leaders in the church; we run community youth clubs which are linked to the church. It would be hard not to mention it and also I didn't want to have to hide that part of me. We decided to be as open as possible about it right from the start.

As it turned out, they weren't at all put off by the fact that we were Christians. The only question they asked us was what would happen if our child turned around and decided they didn't want to be a Christian, what would we do? We answered the question in the way they seemed satisfied with (about free choice and supporting them and loving them no matter what they chose to do with their life) and that was that.

Finally the interview came to end and I could feel myself breathing a massive sigh of relief and relaxing, I was ready to get out of the room, I was mentally fatigued.

The Social Workers said they would have to write up the interview and then show their manager. If they felt all was okay they would let us know within a week by letter if they were going to accept our application to adopt. If they approved our application, then the next stage would be to go on to an adoption preparation class, which were four day sessions. The next ones available for us would be in November. I was a bit disappointed to hear we would have to wait 4 months to get started, but at least we were making progress.

I went in to the interview reasonably confident that we would be approved to go onto the process, but came out of the interview very unsure. I didn't think we did anything particularly wrong but they were very hard to read and I had no idea what they thought of us.

We walked to the car, a bit dazed by the interview. As we were chatting about what we had said and how we felt it went my phone started ringing. I picked up my phone, thinking it would be my parents asking how the interview had gone, but it was from a private number.

"Hello?" I answered.

"Hello is that Pip John?"

"Yes it is" I replied, still none the wiser who was calling.

"Hello Pip, it's Jenny, the senior Social Worker, from the interview."

"Oh hi Jenny." I wondered if we had left something in the room and had to go back, surely they didn't need any more information off us, they couldn't possibly have anything left to ask. I signalled to Stacey to slow down or turn around.

"Pip, I have just seen my manager on the stairs. I had a quick chat with her about your application. We were very impressed with you and Stacey and would really love to have you start the process. You did an excellent interview and think you would be great. We would also really like it if you could join our course starting in September so we can move your application through as quickly as possible.

Do you think you would be able to get the time off work?"
I just sat there stunned, I couldn't believe it! My mind
started whirring. As Jenny reeled off the four dates in
September that the course would be on, I was still
computing the fact that they liked us and, not only did
they like us, but that they wanted to fast track our
application. It was such a confidence boost, and finally the
feel good factor came in abundance. I started to feel the
excitement mounting. We had done it; we had got onto
the course! I know it was just the start but to me it was a
major step. I told Jenny that those dates would be
absolutely fine and we would love to start the classes in
September. She said she would send us the details and we
ended the call.

I looked at Stacey and told him what they had said. He
couldn't believe it either. He looked at the clock and
commented that instead of waiting a week to find out, we

actually heard within 7 minutes of the interview ending! It was amazing, exciting, nerve racking, fantastic. This was it, we were actually doing this; we had been approved! It turned out that that first approval was the first of many approvals needed on this adoption journey.

Chapter Nine

September 2011

Adoption Preparation Classes

Fortunately I have a very supportive work environment and getting those days off for my preparation classes was not a problem. I work as an Audiologist in the local hospital and we book patients up to six weeks ahead in our diary so in order for me to get three days off at such short notice was quite hard but they arranged it for me with no problems. The path was set clear for us to attend the adoption preparation classes.

My feelings about the adoption classes were that I was excited to get going, to finally be doing something positive towards getting closer to adopting our child.

I'm going to be honest about the adoption classes and say that I felt about 60% was useful and the rest was not. Now, as I've said before, adoption is a very personal journey and everyone is different, so I expect there will be people who disagree with this and found it all very helpful. The Social Workers were very good and the presentations of the classes were varied, with different people doing different things. I imagine it would be difficult to set a class to fit the needs of everyone so they did the best they could to make sure everything was covered.

I've told you that I am quite an indecisive person; well I am also quite shy. In group situations I tend to sit back and let others talk. So in some ways I was quite nervous about these classes. I was unsure what would be expected of me and I'd heard bits and pieces from people about what to expect. The area I was most dreading was the role play. As soon as I hear the words role play, I start to panic and my heart sinks. I try to think of ways to get out of it; role play is my nightmare. I don't know if it is a confidence thing or just that I hate being centre of attention, particularly when it is in front of a group of people who I don't know. So, I was not looking forward to that part. The only positive was that Stacey is very comfortable being centre of attention and being the life and soul, so role play to him would probably have the opposite effect, he would be excited at the prospect. (As you can see we are very opposite in personality; it is very true when they say opposites attract). I often find though, that no matter how awful you think something might be, the reality of it is, it's never that bad.

I think the best part of the adoption course were the visits we had from people who had already adopted. It was good to hear about their journey, what was involved and how their children adapted to their new home. It was still all very new and daunting to us so it was good to hear some positive stories.

The sessions on attachment were also helpful and insightful. Attachment is mentioned a great deal in the adoption preparation classes. It is something they want to make sure you understand when going through the adoption process. A lot of the looked after children needing adoption come from very damaged backgrounds and have suffered from abuse and/or neglect. In some cases, this can lead to the children not attaching to their adoptive parents, or if they have suffered abuse from a male, they may not attach to the father figure or vice versa. They were keen to make sure we knew what attachment was and how to deal with it if your child does not attach to you. Again, emphasis was put on the fact that the children who need adopting can be challenging because of what they have been through, and even if you are adopting a young child, they can still struggle to attach.

One area that came up in the adoption course that wasn't so helpful was the discussion on different types of abuse. We spent a lot of time going over that. Now for some people that may well have been helpful. I felt less time could have been spent on this section. This could be due to the fact that we have been youth workers or maybe because I work in the hospital (and therefore get training in safeguarding). It just seemed quite basic and I felt most people would know all about it already.

But the worst part by far was the whole theraplay section. (Not to be confused with play therapy.) I'm not saying that theraplay is not a useful thing to learn about; in theory it does have a part to play, especially maybe for people who aren't confident in how to play with their children. It was how they taught us it that was questionable.

We still tell people to this day about the cringe worthy 'ha ha' activity.

In this activity, we were all told to lie down on the floor (already alarm bells ringing) and to put our heads on the stomach of the person next to you. The idea was that we would all be lying in a circle, each with our head on someone's stomach and someone's head on our own stomach. Now this was already very awkward and embarrassing considering we barely knew these people, but it didn't end there. We were then told to say 'ha' one at a time and depending on where you were in the circle would depend on how many 'ha's' you would say. If you were number one you would say 'ha', if you were number two you would say 'ha ha,' number three would say 'ha ha ha,' and so on. Fortunately I was only number two so only had to say it twice; however to my delight, Stacey was number nine in the group. Now, this was bad enough for me but for Stacey to have his head on the stomach of a man he barely knew and to have another man's head on his stomach would have been his nightmare. You know when you are in a situation where you feel awkward; you know you shouldn't laugh because the Social Worker is taking it very seriously and you don't want to offend. The more you know you shouldn't laugh, the more you want to. As I was picturing Stacey in this position, I started to feel these nervous giggles coming up and it was all I could do to stop myself from laughing out loud. So the Social Worker tells us to start and off we all go,

"Ha."

"Ha ha" (from me).

"Ha ha ha."

On it went until it was Stacey's turn. He had to say it nine times, and I was only just holding it together when I heard his voice;

"Ha ha ha ha ha ha ha ha ha." Hearing Stacey and picturing his face as he was saying those 'ha's' was the funniest experience. They came out in a sarcastic and very monotone way and I tried to crane my neck to see if I could get eye contact, but his face remained resolutely upright. As embarrassing as this was I couldn't help smiling, knowing exactly how he would be finding this. As I lay there, I couldn't actually believe what we were doing. It felt surreal. How was this supposed to help in adopting a child? How was this going to help in dealing with the possible lack of attachment from a child or dealing with challenging behaviour? I really didn't understand it then and I still don't now. There were other cheesy activities we were told to do, which quite frankly just felt quite patronising, like building paper aeroplanes and throwing them at each other, or crumpling up paper and throwing it into the other team's area. Another highlight (not) was when we had to stand in a circle and give each other massages and make movements on their back representing weather.

The role play part of it ended up being a breeze in comparison to all that (and was quite an eye opening session about who is involved in an adoption). We had lots of fun regaling our friends with these very embarrassing moments. (By the way, Stacey later told me he hated every minute of the ha ha task).

I also have to give a mention to the DVD we saw of children who needed adopting. It was quite emotional watching them. The children had different issues for various reasons but it really put faces to all this theory we had been told. It made me feel excited about moving along in the process and being able to help one of those children by providing them with a home.

We learnt a lot of the jargon used in adopting from the adoption classes, like contact - direct and indirect- letterbox contact, life story work, the biological mums of the children were known as tummy mummies, the adoptive mother was known as the forever mummy, and the family unit was the forever family. I couldn't wait to be someone's forever mummy.

We had a short meeting with our Social Worker, Jodie, who would be with us through the whole process. This was someone who would question us on all aspects of our lives and get to know us very well. Jodie was one of the Social Workers who was at our interview and we arranged the first bits of paperwork. (Writing up a family tree, crb form etc).

To my mind, when I think back to the adoption classes, I feel they could have fitted the useful, interesting and informative parts into two or at a push three days rather than the four. Some people may disagree with this and may have felt it was a great way of breaking the ice and learning about theraplay. Everyone is different (and if our group was anything to go by there were people there seemingly enjoying every minute of it). I would have thought a DVD of theraplay and what it is would have sufficed; however, we had to complete it, and complete it we did. We were now ready for the next step; the home study or PAR.

Chapter Ten

September 2011

Attachment Interview

We were told we needed to have individual attachment style interviews. This would be conducted by two Social Workers, our own Social Worker, Jodie, and another. These interviews would be recorded so they could be written up at a later date. We had to do them on our own, so we could be as open and honest as possible.

The result of the attachment interview would reveal our current adult attachment style. There are different types of attachment styles and these determine your quality of close relationships. Once the interview is completed, it is assessed, and you are told what your attachment profile is.

The Social Workers advised us that it didn't really matter what the result was, it just helped them to match a child. So, for instance, if someone came out a markedly withdrawn person, they wouldn't match them to a withdrawn child. The attachment style interviews were held at our home and I was first. I actually felt quite tense, because I didn't have a clue what questions they were going to ask; it felt a bit like an exam, and I just kept hoping I would answer the questions correctly. The questions were about my relationships and how I access my support. I had to mention three people who I was close to and then I was asked the same questions about all three. I chose Stacey, my mum, and my best friend, Claire. The questions were actually quite depressing. Along the lines of, "what would you do if Stacey/your mum/Claire were to die; how would you cope?" "If they weren't there anymore, do you think you could manage"?

Also questions like, "how close are you?" "How do you show how you feel to the people you are close to?" It felt quite intense at the time, mainly because it was being recorded so I was very conscious of the little Dictaphone in front of me. The situation wasn't helped by the fact I had a window open upstairs and every so often the bathroom door would creak closed and then creak back open again. The Social Worker would be saying, "so if your mum passed away, how would you feel?" Then from upstairs, a long creak. I would answer the question and then there would be another loud creak. It was quite off putting. In the end, Jodie decided to go upstairs to find the offending door and close it properly. I finally got through the interview and they told us later in the process that both Stacey and I came out with secure attachment profiles.

Chapter Eleven

September 2011

The Health and Safety Visit

After saying goodbye to the Social Workers following my attachment interview, I had half an hour break and then we had someone coming to do a health and safety visit around the house. This was to ensure our house was safe to have a child living in it. Never mind that the previous owners of the house had two children, we still had to prove that it wasn't a danger zone to live there. I realise why this needed to be done, that the local authority have shared parental responsibility when you first adopt the child. They had to be sure that they were covered so that if anything happened to the child, they couldn't be held responsible. Even though we knew this, it didn't stop us feeling slightly patronised by the whole visit. The lady who did the inspection was nice but she looked around the house and gave all these suggestions how we could improve it and make it safer. I think your home is quite a personal space so it was quite difficult to hear that your house needed to change.

The main areas we were told we had to improve were:

1)   Put a padlock on the shed.

2)   Have a locked door where the confidential files were going to be kept.

3)   Get a gate for our front garden (even though no-one else in our entire street had one!)

4)   Get a hook for the bathroom blind cord to be wrapped around, (even though the cord fell no-

where near where a toddler could reach, let alone a baby).

5)   Make our stair banister higher, it was too low down and could allow a child to fall off the stairs.

All in all, it wasn't too bad a list, most were quite small and easy things to do. The banister was the biggest job and while making it higher, Stacey and I had our first argument since starting the adoption process.

Stacey had put another layer onto the banister to raise its height and had been sanding it down, ready to paint it. It looked absolutely fantastic; he had done a great job. After he had sanded it, I could feel some rough edges. What I hadn't realised was that he hadn't actually finished. I just mentioned that it still felt a bit rough, and did he think that it was ok. Stacey took that to mean that I was criticising his work before it was finished. He got frustrated because he felt I was being impatient and not trusting him to finish the job and make it look nice. He said that as soon as we had got through the adoption process we could do what we liked and take it back down again anyway.

In hindsight, I feel that argument wasn't really about the banister (well it was a bit) but more a release of some of the frustration we had both been feeling. Going through adoption does put strain on a relationship is some ways. I am fortunate that Stacey is a genuinely thoughtful and caring person, and we don't really argue very much. I know for a fact that he would do anything for me and me, him. The health and safety visit was something that Stacey found hard. I think taking time out to make a banister was a pain for him. He works so hard and having to go through so many hoops in order to adopt a child, was starting to get to us both. We are very different people and deal with things differently. I think this argument was just a bit of an outpouring caused by the intense scrutiny we had been under, and things just had to come to a head. The banister was adjusted quite a way down the line into the adoption process, so we had gone through a fair amount of hoop jumping by that stage. It gets very tiring and mentally exhausting trying to prove ourselves to be fit to have children when in our hearts we knew we could do it and were desperate for it to happen. That was banister-gate. (By the way, the banister turned out amazing and looked as if it had always been there).

Chapter Twelve

October 2011-April 2012

The Prospective Adopters Report (PAR)

We had completed the adoption preparation classes, we had sat through our attachment style interviews and health and safety visit. We were now ready for the next step to start: the home studies. This stage was a big part of the process, and I was dying to get on with things and get started with Jodie. We were told we needed eight sessions, once a fortnight with Jodie to go through the PAR. This would cover absolutely everything about us and I mean everything! The first two sessions were individual; we had to do them on our own with Jodie. I felt this was where I could play an active part in getting things moving and bring us closer to more tangible results. Fortunately I had every other Wednesday off work so this fell very nicely in line with the home visits.

Jodie wanted to talk about family origin, other significant partners and identity at our first session. The format would be that she would email me a list of questions around these areas; I would email the answers back to her and we would then discuss them at the home study session.

It started off quite well. I got on well with Jodie and it was quite nice chatting to her about my family and family origin. It didn't really feel like I was being assessed at that point because it was all based on fact, it wasn't my opinion.

Also in our case, we were quite straight forward in these areas because Stacey and I haven't had any significant previous partners to discuss. Both sets of parents are still married and so the family unit was very close, we all get on very well together. In a lot of cases there would be quite a lot of step parents and step/half siblings etc, but for us it was all quite simple.

By session three Stacey and I could do the home study together, which was nice because we had been feeling that we were doing this quite separately. The attachment interviews had been individual as had the first two sessions, so it was nice to get back with Stacey and continue it together.

Session three was all about social and support network. It was all about our friends and family and who we have in our support network that would be helping us when we adopted. Did we have strong relationships with people? Were our parents fully on board with the adoption?

By about session four, I was starting to feel a bit bogged down with all the questions. Every week I would get an email with a list of the next questions, and they just seemed to be getting more and more difficult. I had to spend several evenings just typing up the answers to the questions as some of them required quite a bit of thought. I have to say that if you struggle with paperwork or typing and writing reports, this part of the adoption process can be quite daunting; it is easy to get a bit bogged down with the sheer volume of work needed. Stacey is not that kind of person, so I had to do it all. It also seemed a lot of the questions were repeated. I remember sitting at my computer typing up the answers thinking "I've already told you all this before." I would even look back at some of my previous answers and copy and paste. It seemed a bit of a waste of time, why do I have to keep repeating the same things?

So on it went, question after question; it was quite gruelling. They wanted to know about our health, leisure and recreation interests, criminal convictions (if any), current relationships, accommodation, where we lived, about the area, how long we'd lived here. Also they wanted details about our financial circumstances, motivation for adopting, who we wanted to adopt, access to local services. The hardest (and longest) questions were near the end. I had to give answers to do with understanding expectations about children and the lifelong nature and impact of adoption, experience of caring for children, promoting a child's heritage and identity and on and on. I have to be honest and say in some cases, I didn't even understand the questions let alone know how to answer them. It got really demoralising by then. The last set of questions took me twenty pages of writing to complete! The only thing that kept me going was the thought that I had nearly finished it all.

The plan for home study was to have eight sessions with Jodie to cover all aspects we needed to complete our PAR. We had some fantastic news from Jodie on our third session. She told us that we were doing well on completing the prospective adopters report and they wanted to move our panel date. We had originally been told that our approval panel date would be April but now they wanted to bring it forward to March. We were so pleased; we couldn't believe it. Usually you get told that things are taking longer or there are delays, so to be told it was moving forward felt exciting; we could see the end was in sight. Also, to be told that we were doing well was fantastic.

Jodie gave us some more exciting news. She shared with us that there were three possible child matches for us revealed by what we had talked about. You have to explain the kind of child you want to adopt, the age, sex, race, health: all the important information. They then have a list of requirements and they match those requirements to the children they have ready for adopting. When Jodie told us there were three, I was stunned, I couldn't believe it. After being told so many negative issues, it was great to finally have some good news. We were moving forward. You don't hear what is happening behind the scenes, so to hear there were not one but three possible matches was incredible. I also started feeling a bit panicky and overwhelmed. It all suddenly felt real and was actually happening. Were we ready? Could we do this? It's quite different to think and talk about it but when all of a sudden you are faced with the reality that there are three children matching your profile, it all seemed so scary. Jodie said that once we had our match, it would all go quite quickly, so it looked like we could have our child by May/June!

Jodie left us with our heads and hearts just spinning. Once I had got over the initial panic, I just couldn't stop smiling, I was so excited. It literally put a spring in my step, I was desperate to get going and finish everything off. Moving our approval panel forward meant we had to fit eight sessions into five, which was fine by us, it just all meant that we would get to our goal quicker.

I couldn't stop thinking about the three children that we could possibly be adopting: what did they look like, what ages were they, what were their family situations?

By the end of January we were reaching the end of the home studies. Along with the questions we had already answered, there were quite a few more documents and reports to write. It felt a bit of a slog at the end but we got it all done and in February our last home study session finally arrived!

I was feeling great because I knew things were moving along and I couldn't wait to move on to the next step – the approval panel. Unfortunately, Jodie came to the session with some bad news. The panel date may have to be delayed. Instead of our original March date, it may have to be two weeks later than they thought. Apparently they were very busy with not just prospective adopters but children needing to go through the courts to get their adoption orders. I was so disappointed about the dates being delayed. It was only two weeks but to me for some reason it felt like a lot longer. It was almost as if I had been so fixed on getting to that date, that it felt such a lot further away. Just when you think something is within your grasp, it gets snatched away. I told Stacey and he was more pragmatic about it saying, "It's only two weeks, it will be fine," but I was really upset. I knew I was probably overreacting but I couldn't help it.

I had an email from Jodie asking to confirm we only wanted to adopt one child, (I think we had covered this at least three times already). She wanted to know if we would be prepared to adopt two children if they were both quite young, for example, eighteen months and three years old.

She knew we had our heart set on as young as possible. I emailed back that we only wanted to adopt one child. We felt that as we hadn't had children before, it would be best to start off with one and see how things progressed. If everything went well we would possibly consider adoption again. She was fine with that; I think she just wanted to check. At the time I thought it was a strange thing to ask us because she had already said there were three matches so why would she need to ask about having two children?

We were scheduled a visit with Jodie and a senior Social Worker, Catherine to go through the entire PAR and to make sure everything was ok and to fill in any gaps we might have. I had received another email the day before telling us that our panel date was finalised as being 12th April! I was so disappointed when I received that email because I was still hoping there was a possibility we would be fitted in on the first March date. Not only did we not get that date, we also didn't get the two week later date either. So I started to feel a bit disillusioned with it all. It had been such a long and gruelling process; we seemed to be going one step forward and two steps back. I felt like my entire future was in the hands of the Social Workers. The decisions that they make and the words they say, have impact on our lives. My life was in their hands, they were calling the shots and I felt so out of control. I know it sounds harsh because they had been so great with us; it's just how I felt at the time. It was so frustrating because I like to be in control, I like to plan things and be organised. It was a bit like being back on the IVF journey, where you feel very uncertain about what is happening, and you are not sure what to think because every time you start feeling positive you get a knock back.

Jodie and Catherine came to our house for the meeting and I was still feeling quite frustrated about the situation. I don't like confrontation so I just kept it all in and didn't say anything about it to them when they arrived; just smiled and welcomed them into my home. By nature, I am quite a people pleaser, I hate any sort of conflict or confrontation, and I will do anything to avoid that happening. I am very good at hiding my feelings and just dealing with them inwardly. I am not an emotional person, I would say I am fairly level headed and measured in the way I deal with things. I am not given to outbursts, I definitely don't cry in front of people if I can help it. I try and deal with it myself and move on. I have my moments when I'm on my own. If I need to cry I will do it in private. That's just how I am. I sometimes wish I was a bit more open, but I find it difficult.

I offered Jodie and Catherine a drink and we settled down to go through our PAR. Catherine asked me how everything was going and immediately I felt the tears threatening and did my best to fight them back before attempting to speak. Why did she have to ask that question? It was almost as if my emotions have been on the edge for a long time and evidently this was the moment they would spill over. I tried to answer her question, at the same time fighting back the emotion, but I lost the battle and the tears started to fall. I couldn't seem to stop them. I couldn't speak I was crying too much, this was so unlike me and even as I was crying all I could think of was how awkward it was, they don't want to see me crying on the sofa, get a grip, Pip, I felt so embarrassed. Stacey disappeared into the kitchen to get me some tissues. I think he was quite shocked. He knew I was frustrated with everything but I don't think he expected that reaction, especially from me in front of the Social Workers. He was probably wondering who this emotional wreck was sitting next to him on the sofa.

Jodie and Catherine were very kind and empathised with how I was feeling. I managed to stop crying and apologised for the little outburst. I felt really embarrassed at crying in front of them but they were great, and understood. Catherine tried to explain why the dates had all been moved so much, and I nodded along as she was explaining. I had understood the reasoning before, but, it was just so frustrating, and to be honest I think I was by now mentally exhausted. I had reached a bit of a wall. The rest of the meeting didn't get much better. Catherine wanted to talk about the kind of children that needed adopting, (again going over the difficulties and potential issues there may be). She wanted to talk about the health uncertainties. One condition they talk a lot about is the foetal alcohol syndrome (FAS). She wanted to make sure we were aware that if we adopt a young child there would be a lot of uncertainties about their health. A lot of the birth mothers do have problems with alcohol and drugs and therefore there could be all kinds of issues around that. She went on to ask us what health problems we would be willing to take on and what health issues we definitely would not. Catherine explained that at the moment there weren't any matches for us and there weren't any imminent ones coming through the courts either and so there may well be quite a long wait for us. She informed us that the time from having a match to meeting the child, could be a fair time, possibly up to six months, that it was a long process and we should set our expectations accordingly.

As you can imagine, it wasn't the most uplifting meeting we had ever had. There was a lot of information given which didn't match up to what we had already been told. Mainly that there were no matches, Jodie had already told us of three matches, so what happened to those three?

An issue that we would be facing, Catherine continued, was geography. Because we lived in the same town as the local authority, most of the children needing adopting were from the same town too so we couldn't adopt those children. They match children to adopters who live slightly further afield because they don't want us to risk meeting or bumping into any of the birth family in our day to day living. If we had lived outside of the town, we would have had a lot more choice in who we adopted. (I found out later that that was the reason those three matches weren't right for us).

Catherine obviously felt she needed to be realistic about the situation and let us know exactly where we were with everything. I understood what she was doing but it was difficult to hear. I was quite relieved to get the meeting finished. It was one of my lowest points along this adoption journey. I felt deflated, I felt let down, and I felt frustrated.

It seemed like we couldn't trust what people were saying to us anymore, what was true and what wasn't. It felt one minute we had been told one thing, the next it changed again. Stacey said he would have to wait until we had it in writing or it has been confirmed before he would believe anything from now on.

I had to take a day or two to think about everything we had been told and to try and understand what we were doing and get everything clear in my head. I realised that even though we had suffered a bit of a setback, it was just that, a setback. It didn't change anything. Yes, it was going to take longer than we thought, but that was okay. We had come this far already, it was a journey we were going on; we just had a longer journey ahead. There were a lot of uncertainties but we knew that at the start. So once I had time to think it all through, I realised that everything is in God's hands, he is in control of my life and I trust him completely.

After I had that time I felt so much better and more positive again. I just had to be patient and wait a bit longer and while I was doing that, I was going to enjoy my life and cherish the time I had with my husband. It felt great being back to me again.

The PAR and home study sessions were in some ways difficult but in some ways I enjoyed them. They were difficult because of the sheer amount of paperwork and questions to answer; however, it felt quite empowering because I was at last doing something positive to achieve my dream. I felt a bit more in control by doing something tangible and it felt like things were moving on.

I've heard it said about giving birth, that at the time it is horrendous and painful but once it's done you forget how hard it all was. I felt a bit like that about the PAR: it was difficult, but by the time I had completed it, I had forgotten all about how hard it was and just felt pleased with the end result.

Chapter Thirteen

12ᵗʰ April 2012

Approval Panel

The day had finally arrived, the day we had been waiting for; the day that all our previous hard work had been building towards: the Approval Panel. I didn't sleep much the night before because I was so nervous and excited about the panel. We had been told who would be on the panel and the format. They explained that they couldn't tell us what questions would be asked because they didn't know, however they did tell us the sort of questions that had come up in the past.

The panel had been given our PAR report and had read all about us. They would consider this when deciding if we should be approved for adoption. The panel consisted of a Chairperson, Adoptive Parent/Adoptees/Birth Parent of an adopted child, Educational Psychologist, Medical Advisor, Adoption & Fostering Manager and a Councillor. Also Jodie would be coming in with us.

The plan for the panel was that Jodie would go in first to speak with the panel. She would then come out and we would go in. The panel would commence their questioning. Jodie would be asked to speak on behalf of us, why we should be approved for adoption and what challenges she felt we would face. We would have an opportunity to speak at the end before we left to await their decision in another room. The decision would be made by each panel member casting their vote. The Chairperson would then come out to inform us of the result.

Stacey and I put on our smart clothes and set off for the panel. Stacey was as calm as ever; I don't think he gets nervous about anything. I felt tense and nervous. This meant so much to me, we had done so much to get to this point, and I really wanted the panel to like us and obviously to approve us to adopt. We had been told that very few people get a no at panel; they sometimes get referrals where there are gaps in the PAR that need to be looked into. If we got a yes today it meant we could actually adopt! There would be nothing to stop us. We were so used to keeping a check on our hopes and expectations because of being let down in the past when going through IVF.

Having the approval today meant that, yes, we would somewhere further down the line, have a child. It was such an exciting yet nerve racking time: I just wanted to get through this panel successfully.

When we got there, the Chairperson was waiting for us. She took us through to a waiting area and ran through what was going to be happening. Jodie was there as well and she sat with us. Shortly after the chair went into the panel room, Jodie went to start off the proceedings. About five minutes later she returned for us and we walked in and sat down. It was a strange feeling walking into the room. I looked around and there seemed to be a lot of people sitting watching us. I thought they would be a bit more welcoming, with smiles on their faces, but they were quite serious. I think I saw only one woman who was smiling! We sat down and everyone was introduced, but the meeting was such a blur that I couldn't remember any of their names the minute after they said them. I just remember feeling like I wanted to impress them so they would think we would be great parents. I kept smiling and nodding along.

They started asking their questions and to this day I can't remember much about them. The only one I can recall is how would we deal with a child who didn't attach to one of us? I remember the questions were harder than I had anticipated, and there seemed to be a lot more of them than we were advised there would be. We eventually got through it, answering the questions in the best way we could. We then left the room to await their decision.

It was such a relief to get out and breathe again. There was nothing else we could do now, just sit and wait for the result. Jodie had gone back in to the room, so it was just Stacey and me sitting around a big table. We looked at each other but we didn't really know what to say. We ended up just chatting about mundane things like, was Stacey going to go back to work after this? What did we want for dinner tonight? It was almost as if we were trying not to think of the momentous decision being made in the room next to us.

Eventually Jodie and the Chairperson came into the room to deliver the decision. She said we were going to have a challenging time and we should try and access all the support we could, but was pleased to say their recommendation was to approve us for adoption. The other good news was that the decision was unanimous, they all said yes! We had achieved it! We could adopt! My dream of becoming a mum was getting ever closer. It was an amazing feeling, almost euphoric. I felt immense relief. We could now relax a bit and try and enjoy the rest of the process. We decided to celebrate that night by eating out with my parents. It was a lovely evening, so nice to have something positive to tell people. Our family have been through all this with us, supporting us. All they had heard from us in the past when we were going through

IVF was bad news, and putting them through that is not a good feeling at all. It was fantastic to have some great news to share with them. We had also planned an evening with Stacey's parents at the weekend. We are so blessed to have such wonderful families to celebrate with us in our amazing achievement.

Chapter Fourteen

Life Changes

'What time is it?' I bellowed.

'Mission Impossible!' Came the roar from the crowd.

'I said, what time is it?'

'MISSION IMPOSSIBLE!'

Cue the theme tune from the Mission Impossible films.

This was a typical Friday night for Stacey and me. We were at our youth group and about to start a segment called Mission Impossible. Stacey and I have been youth workers for many years and we had been running this particular youth group for six years. We had a group called Aftershock for age's five to ten and a group called

Riot for elevens and over. The groups ran one after the other every Friday night.

Friday nights had been very hectic for many years for us. It consisted of finishing work at five o clock, rushing home to get changed, picking up some items needed for the clubs, jumping back in my car and picking up a few young people who are helpers for us in Aftershock. I would arrive at the venue for about six o clock, set up for the night (which included tuck shop, and getting the registration area ready), then ready for the start of Aftershock at six fifteen.

Riot ended at nine thirty so then it would be pack down time, take some of the young people home and by about ten thirty all the leaders would go out for a curry/meal. We usually got home at about midnight. It is always quite a hectic night but I loved doing it. I enjoyed meeting the local young people and children and getting to know them.

They were from around the community where we lived and it was very successful. Aftershock was a very energetic full on club, full of games, quizzes, Mission Impossible and a five minute talk. Riot was more of a chill out lounge, with music, PlayStations and sports. Over the six years there have been several leaders come and go but Stacey, myself and my older brother, Marcus set it up and had been there for the whole six years. We have had other helpers as well who came and also, as I've mentioned, in the last year or so, a fantastic group of junior leaders who we had grown close to. They started by attending Aftershock, then when old enough moving on to Riot. They are great young people with whom we had a strong connection. Their enthusiasm to help out led to us making them junior leaders at Aftershock. That was probably the best decision we made. These fantastic junior leaders took the pressure slightly off Stacey, Marcus and I. We actually enjoyed the last year or so more than any other time since we had been running it. It really was a pleasure and honour to be part of such a fantastic team. Some of them also helped us with our adoption process by writing some fantastic references about us and how much they enjoyed the youth clubs.

After six years of running the youth groups, we decided the time had come to stop. It was a very difficult decision to make because it was so successful and we loved being part of it, but there were other things happening in our lives and we just felt the time was right.

Stacey and I really felt that we couldn't continue running it the way we had been as well as going through the adoption process. Our priorities had changed and we wanted to make sure we were ready for whatever the adoption process required of us. Fortunately we found another group from a different church who wanted to take it on, so we were relieved that the children and young people could continue to go to a youth club in their local area.

Our last youth night was December 16th 2011. It was our Christmas party. It was a great night but very emotional knowing it was kind of an end of an era for us. We had formed close friendships with the children and teenagers; we were going to miss them so much. We knew it was the right decision, but it was still very hard.

If you are planning on entering the adoption process, I would encourage you to think about your life and what you are involved with. The process itself is very demanding and takes a lot of time and hard work to complete. It is also mentally challenging. If you have a busy life and involved with a lot of things, you will find it even more arduous. I would really recommend easing off your work load where you can. Your priorities have to change. It will really make a huge difference and when you finally get your children, obviously you will need that time to spend with them.

For the first few months after stopping the youth group, Stacey and I didn't know what to do with ourselves on a Friday night. We felt quite lost and guilty about sitting down watching TV, or going out for a meal; however, it was the nicest feeling not having to run around. It wasn't just the Friday nights that were busy; we had to plan in the week, what we were doing, either it was the talk, the games, or finding a tough challenge for Mission Impossible. It really did free up a lot of time for us which was so crucial.

Even though we loved running the youth clubs, it was fantastic to have the rest and not to hear that Mission Impossible music anymore! We can't watch those films anymore without thinking of Aftershock!

Chapter Fifteen

The Calm Before the Storm

The days and weeks following the approval panel were very quiet. Everything seemed to stop. No more work to do, we just had to wait. We were quite prepared for a long wait because we had been told that were no matches available and none coming through the system in the next couple of months. Stacey and I decided to get on with our lives, try and keep busy and wait patiently for the next step. We went away for a few weekends, visiting my younger brother, Gavin in Devon and visiting my Granddad in Wales. We also went on holiday with the family. At first everything was fine, it was nice to have a rest and not have any more work to do, however, after about a month, I started wondering what was happening, whether there

114

were any matches coming through. I hadn't heard from Jodie for a while and I was keen to hear something, just to know what was happening behind the scenes. Finally early in June, we heard from Jodie. She emailed me to let me know she had some profiles of potential matches for us to have a read through and see what we thought. I spoke to her on the phone and we arranged a time when I could go to collect them. I was so excited to pick up the profiles! I couldn't believe there was more than one. I thought that we were waiting for a match to come through, but I wasn't complaining. It was with excited anticipation that I picked up the profiles from Jodie.

Chapter Sixteen

The Profiles

I took an early lunch at work to go and pick up the profiles from Jodie. This was the most excited I had felt since starting the process. I was desperate to have a look at the profiles to see who we were matched to, and how many children there were. Jodie had emailed to say that she had put a few sibling groups in as well to have a look at just in case we were drawn to any of them. I said that would be fine but at the time thinking we would exclude those as we were quite fixed on having one. I met Jodie and she gave me the profiles. When I saw the pile of documents she had I couldn't believe it. I thought there weren't any matches available? I didn't mind, I just wanted to go and study and read them and see what I thought. I went back to my car and my hands were literally shaking. In my hand could possibly be the profile of our child. It was such an amazing feeling. I was excited but also a bit nervous about looking. I got in the car, and straight away I opened them up to have a look. Jodie had already said that they had put pictures on the profiles but they weren't the real ones. They were just pictures from the internet. Apparently they don't show any real pictures at that stage because they didn't want us swayed emotionally by looking at them. I could understand that, but, I don't know why they put any pictures on at all, I would have just preferred it if they had left them blank. Even though I knew they weren't the actual children, I couldn't help looking at the pictures as if they were the real children; it made me feel quite confused. I had quick look through the papers, there were quite a lot there, about ten. I didn't have time to read them all, but I skimmed through them. There were quite a lot of sibling groups so I put them aside. There were also quite a lot of children older than we were hoping for. Once I had skimmed through them, I put them down and headed back to work. That afternoon dragged slowly by and finally it was time to go home and show Stacey the profiles. The profiles listed their age, any health issues, any abuse they had suffered. It wasn't an easy read. Some of these children were very young and to have to read what they have gone through was extremely heart breaking. Most of the profiles weren't suitable for us. To be honest I was quite puzzled at the time as to why we had been given some of them because they blatantly weren't a match for us based on our PAR. After reading and re-reading them, we finally whittled it down to two. One was a young girl who had been abandoned and left on a doorstep and no one knew any details of any family. She was quite young –

about 15 months at the time of reading the profiles. The other profile we were interested in was a sibling group. Now we had said all along (many times), we only wanted to adopt one child. It's hard to explain but all I can say when I read this sibling profile is that it caught my attention, I couldn't put it down. There was something about their profiles that made me think I wanted them. Bearing in mind that we were only supposed to be adopting one and that was what we had been approved for, I had to push it to one side; however it kept coming back to me. It was a case of head and heart. My head was saying no – we only said we would adopt one, how on earth would we manage two? Could we afford it? However, my heart was saying, yes yes yes! I would love to adopt them both. It would mean we would have a family straight away. It was a boy and a girl, which was great, they would have each other, they were a mixed race sibling group, they were both young, (thirteen months and three years old). I just wanted to do it, that's all I can say. My mind was going nineteen to the dozen, trying to work out if we could manage this! It would mean they would have to have their own bedrooms; we would have to get another room ready. (We had already started thinking about a baby room and what to get etc). I asked Stacey about it and his thoughts were similar to mine, saying that if we did it, it would have to be for the right reason. We still had this other little girl we were quite interested in. Stacey said we would need to find out more before making any decisions about it. We both knew it would mean a lot more work, but we were going to keep our minds open to the possibility. I have to be honest here and say that as soon as I read their profile, I knew I wanted them. There was something inside me that said, yes, we can do this, they are for us, however, at the time, we had to be sure.

Every time I thought of the profiles, all I kept thinking about was the sibling group. If I started to entertain the thought of having them both, I would get excited and found it hard to contain the excitement. When I told our friends we were considering a sibling group, they all said it was a great idea and that we should just go for it. Their enthusiasm was infectious and I couldn't bear the thought of not having the children.

We contacted Jodie to let her know we had whittled it down to two and we arranged a meeting with her to go through the profiles and discuss in more detail. At the meeting, Jodie wanted to know what we thought about the profiles. We went through them all and explained why we didn't feel each one was for us until we got to the little girl and the sibling group. Jodie explained that the foster carer of the little girl was also interested in adopting her. Because she was an abandoned child, the police were still investigating the situation and it could well be a while before she would be ready for adoption. I must admit, I thought it was strange that she showed us the profile of her in the first place. It seemed she wasn't suitable at all and yet we were still given her as a potential match. That just left the sibling group. I didn't mind too much because my heart was set on these two anyway. I was pleased that the little girl was ruled out because it made our decision that much easier. Jodie went on to say that the profiles weren't exactly correct, that some of the details were wrong. I found this quite frustrating. Firstly, we were given about ten profiles, eight of which weren't suitable for us, based on our PAR. Secondly of the two profiles we thought were suitable, the details weren't correct. This process had had quite a few ups and downs as I've already talked about and I was getting to the point of feeling like a puppet on a string. Why were the details wrong on these profiles? Why did they give us profiles to read and base a very important life changing decision on, when they weren't even correct? When I did actually ask Jodie this, she told us they do it as an exercise to see where we really were, what we really wanted, to see if we would change our minds once we had read the profiles. That didn't make sense to me because I didn't see the point of conducting this exercise to see what we really wanted, when the details weren't even correct! I asked Jodie if she could let us have the real profile of the sibling group so we could think again about adopting them. Jodie didn't have the real full profiles with her but she was able to fill us in on the details that we wanted to know. They were brother and sister, the little girl was two and the baby boy was five months old (at the time of the profiles being read). They were full siblings, they had no reported health issues except that the baby boy had been very poorly when he was born and had to stay in hospital for four weeks. They were in different foster homes, and they both had their care and placement orders ready. This meant they were ready for adoption. After hearing this information it took a few seconds to sink in about how young the baby boy was: five months old! Ready to be adopted! The profile had said he was fifteen months old! I couldn't believe it; we had been told so many times that we couldn't adopt a baby that I had kind of accepted that the child would be over one year old, so to find out he was only five months was an absolute dream come true. The little girl was only two, which meant we would have two children still very young to adopt. It felt perfect; it felt like an answer to prayer. It was what we had been hoping for all along. I couldn't believe how great they both sounded. To have a little girl who was two, who we could play with and have some fun with, a little baby boy, with whom we would be able to share his first birthday and first

Christmas with was just amazing. A boy and a girl, it would mean they would have each other as they got older. It felt too good to be true. It was all I needed to know to make the decision. I wanted to adopt them more than ever now. In the space of literally two minutes I went from being confused and frustrated with the situation, to overjoyed and excited. Your emotions are really all over the place; from moment to moment they can change. Jodie left promising she would let us have a look at their full profiles very soon and then we could decide on whether we wanted to proceed. There was a mention again about the fact that because they were young, there would be a lot of uncertainties surrounding their health and that issues could emerge that wouldn't be known about until they were older, especially the baby.

About a week later I dropped into Jodie's office to pick up the children's profiles. We were going away for a week, so we had time to read them carefully and make a final decision on whether we wanted to go forward with adopting these siblings. In her office, Jodie pulled out the paperwork and told me there would be the real pictures of the children in their profiles. This would be the first time I would see them. Jodie just leafed through the papers in front of me and showed me the pictures so nonchalantly that I could barely take it in. I just saw the faces of my future children for the first time! Something I had been wondering about for so long. I don't think Jodie realised what was going on inside me when she showed me the pictures; it was life changing, it was the most amazing experience ever. Jodie was chatting about something to do with confidentiality. My heart was beating so fast, I couldn't take in what she was saying. I was desperate to leave so I could take another look, to just soak up their faces and memorise what I saw. I thanked Jodie and left her office. In my car I got the pictures out to study them properly. I couldn't stop smiling. They were the most amazing looking children ever. The little girl was a pretty little thing, such a cute little smiley face, blonde curly hair, grey eyes. She was so gorgeous I just couldn't believe it. The little boy was completely opposite in colouring to her, he had lovely dark skin and big brown eyes. He was only a little baby, and seeing his little tiny new-born body just filled me with a surge of affection and all I wanted to do was protect and look after him. It was a special moment for me. It was my first look at my beautiful children and they were so much more than I could have hoped for. I couldn't wait to show Stacey. We read through the profiles together; there was a lot of information given to us on them, all about their background and the family background. I'm not going to go into details about their backgrounds because that will be their story to tell, suffice to say it was quite overwhelming. It made us realise the extent of the situation and how complicated it was. They were both very poorly when they were born due to circumstances out of their control. After reading everything, it made me more determined to go through with it, to adopt these two innocent beautiful children and give them a safe, loving and stable home. I couldn't stop reading through the profiles for the next few days and each time I read them, I learnt something more. It was very enlightening. As well as the history of their families, it also gave us details about their birth weight, time of birth etc, - it was great to have that information, to be able to tell them when they are older about those small but significant details of their birth. After reading the profiles it reinforced our desire to adopt these two children, and we were keen to let our Social Workers know how we felt. This felt like a great step forward. We were reading about real children and their real profiles and we had made a decision that we wanted to adopt them. The question about can we adopt siblings was no longer valid, we had made our minds up, we wanted to take the next step.

We had a bit of setback (another one!) in the form of our Social Worker Jodie having a fall at home and being off work sick for three weeks, possibly longer. We couldn't believe it, poor Jodie! Just as we felt we were making progress, this happened. We didn't hear anything more than that for a few days, and I remember thinking what happens now? Do we just sit and wait? Do any of the other Social Workers know where we are in the process? I had a little panic that maybe these profiles were being shown to other prospective adopters and we might lose out if we waited. In the end I decided to email the manager, explaining our position and asking what would happen whilst Jodie was away. I explained we were interested in progressing further and would we be able to move forward with Jodie on sick leave. Happily I received a reply back saying they were aware of our situation and had assigned another Social Worker, Karen, to work with us until Jodie was back. I was to wait to hear from Karen about having a meeting with her and Catherine regarding the next stage.

Chapter Seventeen

Living in the Moment

I have to say, if you are not careful, the adoption process can take over your life. It is such an intense process with so much to do and think about, it literally can consume your mind all the time. You think about it when you wake up, it's the last thing on your mind when you go to sleep. Because it is such a long process with a considerable amount of time waiting for the next stage to happen, we felt it was important to live our lives in the moment as well as looking forward to the future we were about to embark on. We had a couple of great holidays; we enjoyed being who we were as a couple. There were times when I would feel impatient for the next step, but I also felt it was important for Stacey and I to enjoy our time together and not wish it away. We both knew that when the time came to have our children, our lives were going to change irrevocably (especially having two children!). We wouldn't have this time back again. I would advise people who are waiting for something to happen, or waiting for a dream to come true, to try and be patient and not wish your life away. It may be that you have been waiting a long time and nothing can take your mind off it; it's all you can think about. Try and cherish the in-between times also, to understand and savour what is happening in the moment. If you only focus and plan your future for the goal you are hoping to achieve, there is a risk that you will miss all the special moments that you experience while you are on the journey. It took me a while to realise that, but it was so important for me to apply it in our situation. It was a difficult balancing act because for me, it was something I had been dreaming about for so long that at times I got impatient when there were setbacks and delays. I really did try to make the most of our life together as we went through the process. Going on holidays with Stacey, a holiday with my family - I genuinely enjoyed those times. I learnt to appreciate Stacey and our families, to appreciate our evenings out, the dates Stacey and I went on (especially now that we had our Friday nights back since finishing our youth group). I knew that they would be few and far between when the children arrived. And when they did eventually arrive, our lives did indeed completely change!

Chapter Eighteen

Reality Check

'Hi Pip, hi Stacey, would you like to come through?'
Stacey and I got up from where we were sitting to follow
Karen and Catherine through to the meeting room. We
had heard from Karen and had arranged a meeting to
discuss our next step regarding Sophie and Kallum, the
siblings we were hoping to adopt. I was feeling so excited
about this meeting. We had made the decision we wanted
to adopt these two amazing children and we were looking
forward to hearing more information and to find out what
happens next. After the initial welcome and hellos Karen
asked us how we felt and where we were with the
adoption. We explained we were happy to progress with

adopting Sophie and Kallum. They then started to talk about the children and some of the issues that had been highlighted to them. For Sophie, they told us that there were concerns that she may be hyperactive. She was very active and had lots of energy and just kept going all day. She hadn't been diagnosed with hyperactivity but concerns had been raised regarding this by her Foster Carers. They told us she would take a lot of our energy and be quite a demanding child. They said that was something we would have to consider when making our final decision. The other area of concern was Foetal Alcohol Syndrome (or FAS). One of the doctors who had visited Sophie had asked for her to be assessed for this due to some of her behaviours and possible facial characteristics. However after the assessment it was reported that in two different specialists' opinion, Sophie did not have foetal alcohol syndrome.

For Kallum, Karen and Catherine explained that he was a very poorly baby; he had spent four weeks in hospital after his birth and was still suffering from his symptoms. He was a fractious baby who cried a lot, even after being picked up to be comforted, he cried even more. Concerns had also been raised about his eyes. The Foster Carer had reported that he wasn't focusing on her when she walked into the room; he would jump because he hadn't seemed to have seen her. His eyes had been checked out by a doctor and no red reflex had been seen in either eye. He then went back a couple of months later and they found a red reflex in one of his eyes but not in the other. He was due to go back again to be re-checked. The issue of foetal alcohol syndrome was raised again by Karen and Catherine in regards to Kallum. They explained that he was too young to be assessed for it. There were going to be a lot of uncertainties regarding his development; whether or not he had FAS, and if he did, to what degree. When Karen and Catherine had finished explaining all of this they stopped and asked us how we felt and if we had any questions. It was so much to process; I just didn't know where to start in answering how we felt. It was so overwhelming, all these issues, all these uncertainties, I felt stunned, I felt like I was out of my depth. Could I do this? Could I keep going, after hearing such stark information? The trouble was none of it was definite. There were no guarantees; rather, it was, this could happen, that could happen, they may have this, they may have that. My brain just couldn't focus on anything particular; it was just whirl of information going around and around. I felt very low at that point sitting at that table. To be honest, all I wanted to do was get out. I just couldn't take anymore; I couldn't take hearing any more negative information.

It was a tough session. We went in excited and came out deflated and completely overwhelmed by the enormity of what we could be taking on. Stacey answered their questions; I can't really remember what I said, I know I just sat through most of it just listening. I couldn't think of a single question to ask, but at the same time I felt like I had a million questions to ask. Karen and Catherine told us to go and have another think about everything and talk to each other about it and let them know what we had decided.

Stacey and I left the meeting and walked to the car in complete silence. It was like we were both so stunned, we didn't know what to say, where to begin. We were both just going over everything in our heads trying to make sense of it all. My emotions were near the edge; I could feel them there, just trying to spill out. I felt tired and low and had no energy to talk about it. We drove home in silence. When we got home, it was a nice day, so we sat outside and made a drink. I had their profiles in my hand and was reading through them again with new eyes, reading every single detail. Eventually we had a discussion about it. We talked about how we felt about it all. We had to be honest with one another and tell each other the truth. I told Stacey that I was having doubts about it all, that I wasn't sure if could do it. It felt too big, too much. He said he wasn't sure either; we had to take time to think about it, to make the decision not based on a reaction to the meeting. We talked about what our deepest fears were and if we could we deal with those fears? If we could, then we could get through everything else. Once we started talking about it, all the questions that I hadn't asked suddenly came to me. What was a red reflex? What did it mean? Did it mean he would be blind in one eye? Was there surgery to rectify it? How old before you can test for

FAS? How severe did they think the FAS could be? And so on. The trouble was I don't think there were any answers to all of the questions. The whole point of adopting is that there are so many unknowns, so many issues that may not be answered until they are older. Stacey had to go back to work and once he had gone, I admit I had a cry on the sofa at home. I felt sad; I felt like I wished I had never started this journey. I cried for the fact that I couldn't have my own children; I wanted my life to be straight forward and easy. Why couldn't I just fall pregnant? I don't know if I was strong enough to cope with all of this. It was a difficult day. After a while I rang mum to tell her how the meeting went, but she wasn't in and I spoke to my dad instead. Talking with my dad helped me so much that night, I'm not sure if he even knew how much he helped me. I respect my dad so much, his advice is always spot on. He is a strong man and he helped me to lift my eyes away from the problems and see it in a different way. He didn't try to make any decisions for me, just talked it through with me. One of the things that is hard about adoption is that it feels at times quite clinical, you don't get to meet or see the children until late on in the process. All you have is written paperwork telling you all the information you need about the children and Social Workers telling you what might or might not be. It is so easy to lose the fact that these are little children who need love and stability in their lives. They need someone who will take a risk and become their mummy and daddy. It may mean sacrifices; it may mean a different type of lifestyle to what you had envisioned for yourselves. My dad helped me to see that the children we adopt, whatever the circumstances, will bring their love to our family and to think about that as well as everything else. The phone call helped me so much, and I felt a lot better about everything. I thought long and hard about it all. Stacey and I talked more about it; whether we can take this further. After the initial shock of the meeting I started to feel better again. There were still a lot of unanswered questions, regarding the health of Kallum and his eyes, information that we wouldn't know until a later date. That night I prayed and asked God to give us strength and peace about going forward with the adoption. To help Stacey and I be united and feel strongly that we could do this, that these children were right for us.

What Stacey and I had to decide was could we adopt these children knowing the worst case scenarios? We thought about it logically – Kallum may be blind in one eye - fine we could cope with that. Kallum may have foetal alcohol syndrome. FAS is such a varied syndrome, from mild to severe. They could have one or two behavioural issues, or they could have many behavioural issues. They may have no facial characteristics of FAS but have a lot of behavioural FAS, or vice versa. When I got home from that meeting, I read up all about FAS and couldn't help but study the photos of Sophie and Kallum to see if I could spot any facial characteristics. We decided that we could cope with FAS. We chose to accept that Sophie did not have FAS. The specialists had concluded their assessment saying in their opinion she did not present with any positive symptoms of FAS. So that was good enough for us. Sophie being hyperactive, we could cope with that. It may mean needing a lot of energy to keep up with her, but we felt we could do that. There's only so much logical thinking you can do. At the end of the day Stacey and I had to be sure these children were right for us, not logically but in our hearts, did we have peace that these were our children? After the initial wobble, I was one hundred per cent determined that we were going to adopt these two wonderful children. I didn't know what the future was going to hold but I knew in my heart that I had to adopt them, that I was going to be their mummy. Stacey and I had always said to each other we wanted to adopt a baby, as young as possible. Whoever we chose to adopt, there would always be uncertainty due to their age. I made the decision not to dwell on all the uncertainties, I was just going to celebrate the fact that these two gorgeous children would be coming home soon, would be coming to start their new lives with us and I was excited. Now all we had to do was convince their Social Workers that we were suitable adopters for Sophie and Kallum.

Chapter Nineteen

July 2012

Meeting the Children's Social Workers

I had emailed Karen explaining that we were happy to move forward in the adoption of Sophie and Kallum and she explained the next stage was to meet with their Social Workers. By this time, Jodie was back from her sick leave and it was good to reconnect with her to arrange some meetings.

Our first meeting was with Charlie, Sophie's Social Worker. We had arranged that he would come to the house, along with Karen and Jodie, Stacey and I. I felt this was quite an important meeting because Charlie knew

Sophie. This was the first person we had met who actually knew the children, not just seen paperwork or profiles, but actually knew her, knew her personality, knew what her needs were. So I felt quite nervous about meeting Charlie, I wanted him to be impressed by us, to think that we were the best people to adopt Sophie. I was at home, waiting for everyone to arrive; Stacey hadn't got back from work yet so I was a bit nervous that he wouldn't be here before Charlie arrived. My fears were realised because about ten minutes before the scheduled meeting, the doorbell went and Charlie was the first to arrive. I kept praying that Stacey would turn up any minute; I just thought it looked bad that Stacey wasn't here when Charlie arrived. I was eager to please and thought that first impressions were very important. Stacey arrived a few minutes after Charlie, apparently there were some major traffic works going on and it took Stacey twice as long to get home. I made

Charlie a coffee and he was asking questions about when we had been approved for adoption and how we were feeling etc. He was walking around the house looking at everything. I was following where he was looking checking it was clean and that the house looked nice and child friendly. He kept going over to the windows and staring out and saying things like "it's very quiet around here". I would follow him to the window and look out and wonder what on earth he was staring at. My eyes would flick up and down the road in alarm, in case something unsavoury was out there. The way he said 'quiet' felt quite ominous. Was it a bad thing to be quiet? I looked out the window again with him, thinking; "It's Monday afternoon; everyone's at work or school, so of course it's going to be quiet!" What did he expect to see, a big brass band walking up and down our road? It was perplexing. Charlie was giving nothing away. After a while of looking around

147

the house and a lot of gazing out the windows (front and back - both quiet), Jodie thankfully arrived along with Karen. Introductions out of the way, we got down to business.

Charlie asked us some questions about us, why we felt we wanted to adopt Sophie and Kallum. He told us a bit more about Sophie, how she was a cute little thing, very affectionate and lovely and loves to give cuddles. She was used to a big busy house, and was full of beans. He told us a bit about her background and the foster family she was with. He felt because she was in a busy environment, she wasn't getting much attention, and in a way she had to fight for some attention. He didn't feel she was hyperactive but just that she was in an environment with quite a few other older children and so had to be quite lively to keep up with them all. He felt that if she were to be adopted by us, she wouldn't need to fight for attention and so we would notice a big change in her behaviour. She would get a lot more attention from us than she had been at her foster home. It was actually so refreshing to hear positive information about Sophie. His perspective was obviously very different from the other Social Workers; he wanted us to know how lovely and great Sophie was and what a pleasure she would be to adopt. He didn't mention anything negative about her at all. It just made me even more excited about meeting her; it couldn't come soon enough for me. Charlie didn't really give away much as to what he thought of our suitability to adopt Sophie; he was perfectly courteous and informative but just hard to read. I asked him at the end if he wanted to ask us anything about ourselves but he just said he needed to chat to the team involved and would let us know in due course. The meeting finished and they all left, with one more mention from Charlie about how quiet it was around here. They promised to be in touch soon. I was so excited; it was so nice to have a positive meeting for once, to end a meeting and not feel low or upset. I felt elated and really hoped that Charlie liked us. I have to say that I wasn't sure what Charlie thought of us at that stage; he was a very hard man to read, part of me thought he wasn't very impressed by the house or the fact that is was so quiet. Next time we were to meet with him, I decided I'd have to arrange for my parents and Stacey's parents to come and visit one after another so he didn't think it was so quiet. If he wanted busy and noisy, we could give him busy and noisy!

As it turned out, Charlie was more than happy with us. He thought we would be ideal adopters for Sophie and thought our relationship was one of the most secure relationships he had ever encountered in his job. He got all that from a half hour meeting! I was over the moon. Although I found Charlie hard to read at our first meeting, he turned out to be one of our biggest advocates throughout the rest of the process and we had a great relationship with him. We have a lot to thank Charlie for.

The next meeting was with Kallum's Social Worker, Alicia, who was a newly qualified social worker so she came to the meeting with her supervisor. I wasn't as apprehensive about this meeting, because Charlie's meeting had gone well, therefore I felt more relaxed at this one. Also because Kallum was only a baby, Alicia had only met him twice, I didn't feel the pressure as much. Alicia told us at this meeting that Kallum was progressing very well. His eyes seemed to be much better; he was focussing well and following people around the room. He hadn't had his red reflex checked again but when given special cards for testing fixing and following he did it very well with both eyes, so they were pleased with his progress. He was also sleeping a lot better, smiling a lot more, a much happier baby than when they last saw him. In their words they felt as though he had turned a corner. We were thrilled to hear such great news again about Kallum, it just reinforced the peace that we had about adopting him. I was desperate to see another photo of Kallum because we had only seen one of him just after he was born, so he would have changed so much since then. I felt so close to them, it may sound strange, but I felt maternal towards both of them, and I hadn't even met them. Again, it was a positive meeting and I was so pleased with the result. Alicia said she was happy for us to adopt Kallum. I was feeling so happy; everything was just clicking into place. We had approval from the Social Workers, another big hurdle jumped. It was a great time for us in the process.

The next step was meeting Sophie and Kallum's Foster Carers.

Chapter Twenty

August 2012

Meeting the Foster Carers

Sophie and Kallum were at different foster homes, so that meant meeting two sets of Foster Carers. I must admit by now, I was getting quite tired of meetings. We had had so many by this stage; however, I was happy to go along with it, if it meant we were closer to adopting the children.

It is quite unusual for siblings to be in different foster homes; usually they try and place siblings together. The reason they weren't in the same place was because Sophie's Foster Carer already had three foster children (two of whom were Sophie and Kallum's half brother and sister). They also have three children of their own as well as the grandfather living there, so as you can imagine it was quite a full house. When Kallum was born they felt he needed a lot of care and attention so decided to place him with a single Foster Carer. The plan would have been that when he was up to it, to move him in with Sophie and the others. In the end, because we had shown an interest in adopting Sophie and Kallum, they didn't feel it would be in Kallum's interest to move him to Sophie's foster home, only for him to be moved again to us. They felt it would be an unnecessary upheaval for him.

These meetings were felt to be a good idea to give us an opportunity to ask any questions we had about Sophie and Kallum, to find out any more information about them. We would have the opportunity to ask them about their routines and their personalities. To ask how the Foster

Carers felt about their development, even to ask about what sort of food they liked/disliked.

The first meeting with Sophie's Foster Carers was set up. I felt quite nervous about the meetings, because even though we didn't need their approval as such, I still wanted them to feel happy about who was going to adopt their foster child. It felt a bit awkward to start with because we were coming from different angles. They would be losing a child; we would (hopefully) be gaining a child. It felt a bit strange. As soon as the meeting started it became apparent that these Foster Carers were very good and happy to fill us in on all the information we wanted. They told us all about Sophie and what she was like. It was a very informative session; we learnt a bit more about Sophie and the picture I had in my head was coming together nicely. Most of it was positive but there were areas of concern about the hyperactivity. They warned us she was very active and lively. We didn't hear anything we hadn't heard before, so that didn't bother me too much by that stage. We were prepared for that. For us personally, we found it a great meeting because we found out that they took Sophie to church every week and they prayed together every night. It is something that we would be doing with Sophie and Kallum so it was wonderful to hear that Sophie was used to going to church every week. I think the Foster Carers were pleased to hear that we also went to church and it was very much a part of our lives. It was a positive meeting and it just made me realise looking back throughout the process that God's hand has been in this the whole time and it just re-confirmed to me that these were meant to be our children. We then met with Kallum's Foster Carer. This was also a great meeting. It was lovely to hear about Kallum's progress and how well he was doing compared to when we had that meeting with

Karen and Catherine. She had no concerns about his health. She told us he was a happy baby, slept well, loved attention and playing. She had written down his daily routine for us so we could carry it on when we had him. She was very organised and we could tell she was an excellent Foster Carer and loved her job. It was just amazing to hear how well Kallum was doing compared to how poorly he was just a couple of months ago. Both meetings were positive; it finally felt we could start to get excited about it all, there was going to be no new surprises that we didn't already know. We had all the information we needed and from now on, only positive feedback was coming through. It felt great. We at last began to see the light at the end of the tunnel. The time had nearly come for us to start our family. We had our date for the matching panel; 12th September 2012. We still had a little way to go, but we were on the home straight.

Chapter Twenty One

September 2012

The Matching Panel

The day had finally arrived. The next big approval we had

been waiting for; the matching panel. This was where we

sit in front of yet another panel and answer questions

about our suitability to adopt Sophie and Kallum. We had

had a meeting (yes another one) previously with Karen

and Jodie to prepare us for what to expect from the panel.

What sort of questions to expect. They gave us advice on

what to say and what not to say. They told us to be humble

and not come across as too confident (that wasn't hard)

and not to presume that we would be matched. We had

been prepped and we couldn't do any more, the day had arrived.

On the day of our approval panel back in April I had felt nervous, but the feeling I had on the day of the matching panel was emotional. I can only explain that from the moment I woke up, I felt incredibly emotional. It was like a culmination of everything that had gone on before. All the ups and downs, all the wobbles, all the doubts, all the excitement had led us to this day. It felt like there was a lot more riding on this. This meeting was more personal because it was about Sophie and Kallum. I felt like I knew them; I felt like they were our children already; it was so important to me that we were matched to these children. It was unthinkable that we wouldn't be matched and would have to start again with different children. I had been thinking about Sophie and Kallum for so long and planning our lives together that I know I would be devastated if we had a no. I am a big believer in everything happening for a reason and I strongly felt that we would get a yes because of everything that had happened. I knew God's hand had been in it and that he had led us to Sophie and Kallum. That didn't stop me feeling emotional. I just wanted it so badly; I could feel my dream was within my grasp, all I needed was this final yes.

The panel consisted of the same people as our approval panel, give or take a few. We had Charlie come through with us, Alicia was supposed to be there, but she was on sick leave, so Charlie was going to speak on her behalf for us. Jodie was also there and Karen. Karen had given me some tissues in case I needed them. She knew what this day meant for me. We were told that the first question was going to be why do you want to adopt Sophie and Kallum? I had said to Stacey that I would answer the first question and then he could answer the next. So we agreed on that.

As we went in and took our seats, one of the members of the panel asked us the first question. "Would you like to tell us why you want to adopt Sophie and Kallum?" I opened my mouth to answer but couldn't. The emotions were too strong. Talking about Sophie and Kallum made it all very personal and I just felt so overwhelmed by it all. I looked at Stacey to try and telepathically tell him he had to answer. He got it immediately and answered the question. I took a sip of water and my hands were shaking. I needed to get a grip, this was important. By the time Stacey had finished answering, I felt calmer and more in control. I was ready to answer the other questions.

We were asked about how we were going to adapt our lives to have two children, how we would manage childcare, what our work plans were, what kind of support network we had (very good). They also asked about our finances, what qualities we had to make us suitable to adopt two children rather than one. They wanted to know why we had changed from wanting to adopt one to adopting two. We managed to get through the panel questions. They then asked the Social Workers various questions and gave them an opportunity to speak on our behalf. They all and spoke highly of us, especially Charlie, who was great and told them we would make fantastic parents to Sophie and Kallum. He informed them how impressed he was with us and how secure we were as individuals as well as a couple. I was so grateful and touched hearing those words, considering we had only met him on one occasion. He talked as though he had known us for years. At the end we were asked if there was anything we wanted to add. I tried to convey how important this was for us, how much we wanted to adopt these children, how passionate we felt about Sophie and Kallum. I struggled to get through it because by the end my voice cracked and I had to stop. They nodded and smiled as I spoke, and we got up and left the room.

We were back in that same room, waiting for the result. Charlie, Karen and Jodie had stayed in the meeting room to discuss any other questions the panel had. I felt good, I felt it went well, but the anticipation was killing me - I just wanted to know. After what felt like ages (but was probably only about five minutes) they came out. The Chairperson told us that they had all voted and we had a yes. It was unanimous! They recommended we were to be matched for adoption to Sophie and Kallum. It was such an amazing feeling. The relief was immense. We had done it; we had got our yes which meant we were going to be parents to Sophie and Kallum! It was amazing, we were thrilled. It was the best day so far in the process. I was thankful to Karen for the tissues because they indeed came in handy in that moment!

Karen explained that even though we had been recommended to be matched, we still had to wait for the official yes, which would take up to three weeks. It's unbelievable that after we get the yes from the panel we still had to wait another three weeks to have it made official, three weeks! They explained they couldn't guarantee the match until we had the official yes, so we had to wait before anything else could happen. Despite this, they asked us to get the rooms prepared and gave us a list of items to get ready. We had to make a welcome book for the children, photos to show the children, clothes from us to give the children. So after getting the rooms ready and spending all the money on the furniture, they could still turn around and say no. It didn't really feel fair; however, I was confident by then that we would get the official yes, so I set about getting the rooms ready.

As we drove home from the matching panel, I couldn't help but think that Sophie and Kallum were our double blessing. We came to this adoption process, fully intending to adopt one child and now we had the privilege of adopting two beautiful children. As I was thinking of this, my thoughts drifted back to the 'long way round'.

The long way round was a message I had heard at a women's conference I had attended a few years back. Some women from my church had organised a trip to this conference. It was just before starting my third cycle of IVF. A lot of people who go to a conference like this go hoping to hear from God, to get encouragement or to feel closer to God, maybe get some answers to things that they are praying or hoping for. I, however, was the opposite about this conference. I deliberately said to God that I didn't need to hear anything, didn't need to feel challenged about anything or encouraged. I felt okay with my situation, I knew that this was God's plan for me, to be going through IVF, I didn't need any answers. I just wanted to go and have a nice time with some friends from church and just enjoy being at the conference.

Looking back I realised I was putting barriers up, almost as if I was afraid of what I thought I was going to hear. We all arrived at the meeting venue on the first night and got to our seats. The woman giving the message got up and told us her title of her message was the 'long way round'. She went on to talk about her life and what she had been through. I had been to a lot of meetings in my life and heard a lot of messages but this one was the most life changing for me. It was so specific to what I was going through. Marie started by telling every one of her struggle with IVF and how difficult the journey was for her until she had her two children. As soon as she said the words IVF, I felt butterflies in my stomach, because I knew God wanted to speak to me and I didn't know if I was ready to hear it. Everything she said, was me, everything she felt, was me. She went on to say that some people have to go the long way round and when it seems that people are achieving what you are longing for so easily, you question why it hasn't happened for you. Marie explained that God takes people the long way round for a reason. He has a special journey for those people and along the way those people will receive other blessings and also be a blessing to other people. It impacted me in such a huge way, God just completely spoke to me in a way I had never heard before, it was as if he was saying to me, "I want you to hear this, I have seen your tears, I have seen your heartache, and I understand what you are going through. You don't have to hide your real feelings, and you don't have to be strong all the time". Marie ended up by using an illustration in the bible where there were two miracles; one that was instant and one that took more time to complete. In the miracle that took a long time, it resulted in a double blessing. She finished by saying to all those going the long way round; be strong because you will eventually get your double blessing.

Throughout the duration of the message, I could feel the emotion building inside me and it was all I could do to stop the tears. I sat through that whole message grinding down on my teeth, fighting back the emotion that was threatening to spill over. It was so difficult to sit through; the feelings that went through me were all engulfing. All I can say is that I felt completely overwhelmed by God's love for me. Even though as a Christian I already knew it, it was like it went to a whole other level. I knew it was real because I am not an emotional person and the emotion that came out of me in that meeting; I have never felt before or since. As soon as the message finished, Marie asked the people who could relate to what she had said to stand up. Again I had to fight with myself to stand up. If I stood up people would see it meant something to me, but I couldn't ignore it. I couldn't ignore the fact that God was speaking to me, so I stood up. As she started to pray for people going through IVF, it was too much for me; I broke down and started crying. I just couldn't hold it any longer and it all came out. Fortunately she finished the prayer fairly quickly and everyone sat down. I left the meeting and headed for the nearest private area and just had a good old cry. It felt great to release all that emotion. It was something I needed to hear, and I'm so glad I went to that meeting; despite the barriers I had put up, God still managed to speak to me in such a powerful way. He knew what I needed to hear even more than I knew. That message helped me to deal what was to come in my life that I had no idea about. At the time I thought it was to do with my IVF journey because I was just about to start my third cycle. I half-jokingly thought that the double blessing would be that I would fall pregnant with twins. Oh how wrong I was.

That day in the car after the matching panel, I realised that actually it was Sophie and Kallum who were my very wonderful and special double blessing.

I finished work the following week and had two weeks annual leave before the adoption leave started. In those two weeks I decorated both our spare rooms for our children. We had already sorted out the little room as a nursery. After we passed the approval panel, we decided to get a room ready while we were waiting for the next stage. In our minds at the time we were adopting a baby, so we decorated one of the rooms as a nursery. We now needed to decorate and get the other spare bedroom ready so we could accommodate both children. The two weeks annual leave were probably the loveliest two weeks. The pressure was off, we had got through the matching panel, I had finished work for a year and I had time to get the bedroom ready for Sophie. I was in my element. I loved looking through catalogues and magazines and thinking about what I wanted for Sophie's bedroom. It was a fantastic time; choosing the baby pink paint, putting up the pretty butterfly wallpaper. It was as though at last I could finally do all the things I had longed to do for so many years. I loved every minute of it. Both bedrooms came out lovely. We had a jungle wall mural for Kallum's bedroom and lovely pale pink room with butterflies as the main theme in Sophie's room. It was a real girly girl's room, and I couldn't wait for her to see it and make it her own. I had a bit of a moment when I finished her room and looked around. I had my baby boy's jungle room finished and my little girl's pink butterfly room ready. I just couldn't believe how far we had come, how close we were and how excited I was to see these rooms occupied by our beautiful children. I was longing to hear the house ringing out with the sound of our children's voices and laughter; it was a very special moment for me.

After the matching panel, we were told by the Social Workers to start thinking about doing a welcome book for Sophie and Kallum. The idea was that the Foster Carers would show the children the books while we were waiting for the introductions to start. Then, hopefully by the time we got to meet them, they would be familiar with our faces and the house. Jodie recommended a Tomy photo book that we could record our voices on. On each page, they could hear our voices saying hello, or introducing our house, their bedroom etc.

This seemed quite straightforward, however I had no idea really where to start. I was fine about taking the photos of the house but how would I go about speaking in the book? What would I say? Jodie's helpful words to me were, "you're a youth worker - be creative!" When someone tells you to be creative, all at once, your creativity just disappears and your mind is grappling to find something, anything that could be construed as creative (not that there was much there to begin with). Suddenly I felt this pressure to have the most creative funny, witty, child friendly book. What on earth was I going to do?

The next few days all I could think about was what could I do, how could we make this book good? After searching for this elusive creativity, I hit upon an idea. I decided to incorporate some sort of teddy bear, who would be going on the journey with the children through the house. On every page, this teddy would be somewhere in the photo and also be the voice of the book. The children not only then would see the house and rooms but there would be a game as well, find the teddy in the photo.

I know what you're thinking, all this thought and this was the best I could come up with? Well I'm afraid to say that was the best I could think of in the time I had, and to be honest, I felt quite pleased with myself. It was a relief to have an idea and so I set about getting it done. I decided upon Minnie Mouse for Sophie's book and Mickey Mouse for Kallum. These were cuddly toys bought for them previously by Stacey's mum and dad, so we already had them. The thought was that after seeing them in the book, the children would be happy to see them when they came to live with us. Now that the idea was there, the photos were taken of each room and of Stacey and me, with Mickey and Minnie Mouse appearing in each page.

All we needed to do now was record our voices on each page. Well, could we do it? I can't remember the amount of times we had to delete the recording and start again. We had to make it all fun and cheerful and animated, and each time we did it, just sounded cringe worthy and embarrassing. We would either stumble on our words, or laugh half way through or just completely forget what we were saying. You only had eight seconds per page to say what you wanted to say, and they just seemed to go by so quickly. We did laugh a lot over this and it was quite a fun thing to do in the end, especially Stacey trying to get the right volume. It was either too quiet you couldn't hear it or it boomed out and ended up sounding too scary and probably would have made the poor children cry.

We eventually finished the book. It was still cringe worthy and embarrassing but it was the best we could come up with. As anyone who has recorded their own voice knows, you always sound so different to what you think you sound like. On top of that we had to speak in child friendly animated voices, like this book was the most exciting book in the world! To be honest listening to it back was painful.

I went to meet Jodie to give her the books along with some clothes of ours she asked for to give to the children. (So they can get used to our smell and appear familiar to them when we met). Jodie arranged to meet me in the foyer of her office. I met her there and handed over the bag with the items in. Before she could get the book out of the bag and open it, I said hello and goodbye and started to make my way quickly to the exit. Unfortunately I wasn't quick enough. I looked on in horror as Jodie's hand went into the bag and retrieved one of the books. She opened the book and out came my recorded voice loud and clear for all to hear. "Hello, Sophie, welcome to your new home.

We are your new mummy and daddy and this is Minnie Mouse."

Now let me paint you the picture; we were in a very spacious big foyer, there were no carpets so the acoustics were quite loud. It was a quiet area because there were only a few people milling around and out of the stillness and quietness of the foyer my voice rang out. Was it my imagination or did it just get deathly quiet in here? The few people who were there seemed to have stopped what they were doing to find out where that weird voice came from. Jodie looked at me and I looked at her, and just as I was about to offer an apology for my lame efforts to be creative, she smiled at me and told me it was brilliant. "Oh" I said, relief flooding through me "thanks." She reached down to turn the page, but I really couldn't take hearing anymore. I quickly drew her attention to the clothes in the bag. She seemed satisfied and placed the

177

book back in the bag to have a look at the clothes. I

breathed a sigh of relief, wished her a nice weekend, and

hastily headed for the door.

Chapter Twenty Two

A Chance Encounter

I parked my car up and remarked to my mum how busy it was. I was surprised, I didn't expect there to be queues coming out the main door and snaking around the building. We were at a nearly new baby sale. Two weeks had gone by since the matching panel and we had one week left before we received the much anticipated official yes. Once that had come through, the introductions could start. We would then finally be able to meet the children. I was getting very excited. The three week wait was tough, but because I had so much to do, I got through it. Also it was an exciting time for us; all the approvals had been granted and we knew the children were going to be ours. It was a great feeling to have that pressure off and to look forward to meeting the children.

When a friend of mine told me about this nearly new baby sale, I thought it would be a lovely way of getting some nice stuff at cheap prices. We had already been blessed with most of the items we needed thanks to our generous family and friends (who had given me their presents at a lovely surprise baby shower for me). I was always on the lookout for some bargains though. These were some of the things that I was looking forward to doing; going out looking for baby clothes to buy. My mum came with me to this sale because Stacey had to work. It was lovely having my mum there as I am so close to her and she has been such a support to me throughout the process. I think she was nearly as excited as me to meet the children.

When we got to the venue, there was a long queue so we walked up to join the end of the queue and waited. Nothing seemed to be happening for a while so we were just chatting away to each other about what we were hoping to find, what kind of things I wanted to get. After a short while, the queue started slowly moving. As mum was chatting to me, I suddenly heard a voice nearby that I recognised. It wasn't a familiar voice as in one of my friends but I knew I had heard it before somewhere. It took me a while to place the voice, I didn't want to turn around because I didn't yet remember who it was and I thought it may look a bit rude. I just carried on listening; not hearing what she was saying but racking my brain to think where I had heard her voice. Then it hit me! It was Kallum's Foster Carer, Katie. As soon as I realised that, I was certain it was her. I subtly tried to glance around without actually looking at her. You know the kind of thing, when you are trying to look at someone but desperately not trying to look like you are looking at them. I thought I was being subtle but Stacey says I am about as subtle as a brick, so she probably could see me doing it, however she did say later that she had no idea. As I was (subtly) trying to get a look at her, I definitely recognised her, but I also noticed something else. She had a pushchair with her, which could only mean one thing. Kallum was also there! I couldn't see his face because it was a pushchair that faced towards Katie, so I could only see the back of it. I knew for certain it was Kallum because she only had Kallum in her foster care. I couldn't believe it. Out of all the people that could have been in that queue that day, Kallum was right behind me. I faced forward; I was shaking and I could feel my heart racing! I was absolutely stunned. My son was literally centimetres away from me. I didn't know what to do.

Mum had no idea what was going through my mind at the time; she carried on talking unaware that my world had just suddenly dramatically changed. I managed to answer her questions or chat back to her as best I could, all the time thinking about Kallum behind me. My heart was racing, my hands were shaking. I just literally couldn't believe it. I wanted to tell mum but I thought Katie would hear me. I didn't know what to do, I was desperate to see him, but I didn't want to get in trouble or put Katie in an awkward position by turning around and asking to see Kallum. We hadn't had the official yes yet; I wasn't supposed to see him until the introductions started. What should I do? Should I just pretend I hadn't noticed them and carry on? Should I turn around and speak to her and risk getting her and myself into trouble? I have always been someone who follows the rules, I'm not very good at being daring or rebellious. So I was battling it, I really was.

In the end I managed to find the smallest piece of paper in my bag and scribbled to my mum, 'Kallum is behind us.' I folded the piece of paper and surreptitiously passed it to mum. My mum looked confused as I passed her the paper. She took ages to read what I wrote because it was terrible writing written with a very shaky hand. Eventually when she got it she looked at me, I looked at her. Credit to my mum, she didn't look back; I know she must have been dying to. Meanwhile I was still battling with what to do, the queue was moving along and we were getting nearer the door. In the end I thought, I had to say something, my son was behind me. I couldn't not turn around, it was Kallum! I was desperate to see him and having him so close and not seeing him was killing me. I finally plucked up the courage and turned around and got eye contact with Katie. We both faked the surprised, "hello fancy seeing you here" faces when we were both very aware of each other and neither of us knowing what to do.

In the end I had the most amazing first meeting with my son. Katie was great; she let me have a look and a cuddle. It was breath-taking. It was an emotionally charged meeting. I will never forget that first cuddle with my Kallum. It was the most unexpected incredible joyous moment. He was gorgeous, with the most amazing soft curly brown hair and big brown eyes. When I picked him up for a hold I looked into his eyes and I thought my heart would burst. It was all I could do not to cry. All three of us - mum, Katie and I- were close to tears; it was simply amazing! Quite surreal actually because there we were standing in the entrance of the nearly new sale having this momentous meeting, while everyone else was streaming in around us as if it were just another day, just another sale.

I tried to ring Stacey to tell him but I couldn't get through. It was such a shame that Stacey wasn't there that day but I thanked God for my special first meeting with Kallum. It was like a special treat for me, just to keep me going for that final week of waiting. I couldn't concentrate for the rest of that sale. I was still shaking, my heart was still racing. I just couldn't believe it. I did manage to buy some stuff, and Katie recommended some things that Kallum liked, however, I just wanted to leave so I could talk to mum properly about it. I was also dying to speak to Stacey to let him know what had happened.

The week that followed that first meeting with Kallum was amazing; I kept thinking and picturing him, and remembering our first cuddle. I was walking on air and couldn't keep the smile off my face!

I'm sure I don't need to say at this point how even more excited I was for the introductions to start; I just wanted to meet Sophie now and start our lives together.

Chapter Twenty Three

October 2012

Introductions

"Dear Mr and Mrs John,

In accordance with the Adoption Agencies Regulations 2005 I am required to notify you that having considered the recommendations of the Adoption Panel, which met on the 12th September 2012, I have decided that Sophie and Kallum should be placed for adoption with you.

I send you all my very best wishes for the future."

Yes! We had finally received the long awaited official letter. We were now (officially) allowed to celebrate.

Receiving the letter meant we were now able to start the introductions. The very next day we had an introductions planning meeting. Everyone involved met up to plan the next couple of weeks where we would be visiting the children until placement. The introductions usually last for about seven to ten days depending on the children and how it goes. It was slightly more complicated for us because the children were in different foster homes. At the end of the introductions, placement would take place where the children would move in with us permanently.

The people involved in this meeting along with Stacey and I were the Foster Carers of both Sophie and Kallum, our Social Worker Jodie, the children's Social Workers, Charlie and Alicia, and finally Karen and Catherine, who were going to be chairing the meeting.

The meeting lasted a couple of hours and we managed to come up with a time table for the next seven days. At that point we would meet up to discuss how everything was going and plan the rest of the introductions and placement.

When the meeting had finished, the first scheduled visit was arranged for the same day in the afternoon. The first visit was to meet Sophie just for an hour shortly followed by meeting Kallum.

Finally the time had come. The time we had been waiting for, for so long. We were going to meet the children. Obviously I had already met Kallum but Stacey hadn't and neither of us had met Sophie. It was going to be a fantastic day; I couldn't wait to get going.

It's hard to describe how I felt during the introductions. It's such a surreal time. It is very emotional, as well as quite awkward. You feel you are being watched. It is not a natural environment. How well it goes is very much dependent on the Foster Carers. They can make things very easy or very difficult for you. In the main part our Foster Carers were great; very helpful and supportive of us. But even though we had great Foster Carers, it was still a very strange time. We had met our children, but we couldn't be completely normal because there were other people there who had been their main carers, so we were very much in their territory. At times it felt like we were walking on egg shells not really sure what to do and on our best behaviour. It was a very weird dynamic and very exhausting, mentally, emotionally and physically. I would advise anyone going through this, not to have anything else going on at the time, no other work or social commitments; it takes up all of your energy and any spare time you have, you need it for yourself, to unwind. It was even hard work just to make dinner for the evenings we were at home. I have a wonderful mum who made me a few lovely homemade dinners, so we were able stock up our fridge with food and not worry about it. It may seem like a small thing, but it made a massive difference to me during the introductions. The other bit of advice I would give anyone during this time is get as much sleep as much as you can!

We had a little spare time before our first visit to Sophie so Stacey and I decided to drive somewhere close to where she lived to have our lunch. That way we would be nearby, ready for the meeting. I struggled to eat very much at that lunch. I was so excited, apprehensive, nervous. How would Sophie be with us? Would she understand what had been going on? She was two and half, still very young to understand everything. Also there was an added dimension because she lived with her two older half siblings. Would the siblings understand what was happening? How would they feel at hearing that

Sophie was going to be adopted and therefore leaving?
How would Sophie feel about leaving her brother and
sister to live with us and Kallum who was younger than her
and who she didn't know? She had had some contact
visits with him but not very much. It was going to be a
complete change for her and it would probably take her a
while to adapt to the new environment and to bond with
us.

It was with all these questions in my mind that we
approached the door of Sophie's house. We knocked and
waited. I wasn't sure who I expected to answer the door
but I didn't expect it to be Sophie. The front door had a
panel of distorted glass, so you could see movement and
colours but not make anything else out. While we were
waiting at the door, we saw a little person coming to the
door and the colour yellow. I realised it was Sophie
behind the door and my heart started to race, we were

about to meet our beautiful daughter! Wendy her Foster Carer helped Sophie open the door and I looked down expectantly at her. What I saw was this beautiful vision in a bright yellow dress, curly golden hair and the most amazing grey/blue eyes smiling shyly back at us. She was the most beautiful, cute, petite little girl I had ever seen. You may think I was biased but she really was such a pretty little girl. She looked at us, still smiling and the way I would describe my feelings at that moment was when people talk about their heart bursting with joy, or heart swelling with happiness. That is literally how I felt in that moment. My heart felt so full, I could feel it swell inside; it was amazing, and it was a physical feeling. I felt so proud that this was my daughter. I had been waiting for this moment for so long. She was very friendly, affectionate, and smiley. Sophie seemed genuinely excited to see us; you could tell she was expecting us. She had our photo book with her and our pictures that we had given to the Foster Carers. She was absolutely adorable. I felt so blessed, we couldn't have chosen any better ourselves, we really couldn't. Wendy referred to us as mummy and daddy in front of Sophie right from the start, so she called me mummy right from the word go, which I was quite surprised about. I had imagined that Wendy would be called mummy because she would have been too young to understand. It thrilled me to hear those words from her when speaking to me. I just couldn't believe it had happened so soon. We had a wonderful hour with Sophie that afternoon and we left on cloud nine. I was very emotional and also quite overwhelmed by it all. Sophie was amazing. Could we be the parents she deserved? Could we give her the life she deserved?

We left Sophie's house to go straight to see Kallum. I had already met Kallum so was very excited to see him again.

It's strange, because your brain has to switch from being in toddler mode to baby mode, with all that entails. Things like sterilising bottles, feeding, sleeping, and changing nappies; all the routine that goes with having a baby. At first I felt a bit out of my depth because we didn't have any practical training on adopting a baby. Obviously I didn't get any of the ante-natal appointments that pregnant women get to help prepare them. I was just going on what I knew, what I had picked up from friends and family who had already had children and my own research. It was great to see Kallum with Stacey. He was such a handsome little boy, who smiled a lot and was happy to be held by us. It was thrilling to be able to adopt a young baby.

On our first visit we were allowed to feed him his bottle. That in itself was a bit of an experience. Kallum's Foster Carer Katie showed us how to hold him and how to hold the bottle and then left the room to give us some space.

That was very thoughtful of her; however, we really didn't have a clue what we were doing.

Stacey had a go first, picked up Kallum and rather awkwardly held him in his arms.

"Am I doing this right?" he asked me doubtfully.

"I don't know, I think so," I replied

"He's wriggling, what shall I do?"

"Try moving your arms a bit."

"Like this?" Stacey started jerking his arms about rather weirdly.

I started laughing; it was so obvious we didn't have a clue! Talk about in at the deep end! We were very aware that Katie was in the room next to us probably listening.

Suddenly Kallum was sick (not surprising really), Stacey looked up at me in alarm.

"Quick get something, he's been sick!"

"What shall I get?" I started desperately searching for a cloth or something lying around I could use to wipe the sick.

"I can't find anything, shall I get Katie?" I started laughing again as I watched Stacey's face trying to deal with sick on his shoulder and arm.

"Just take him so I can clean up." Stacey held Kallum up towards me to take. I took him and tried again. Kallum started to cry, his milk wasn't normally this stressful to drink, poor thing.

Katie must have heard Kallum crying and came back to check we (or more to the point, Kallum) was okay. She gave us a muslin and we tried again. It was quite comical really. It felt a bit awkward being in someone else's home feeding Kallum for the first time. Even though Katie wasn't in the room, we were aware she was only next door so it wasn't natural. We got there in the end however and after Kallum was fed we played with him with his toys and had a lovely time with him. We could see there was something wrong with Kallum's left eye; it kept floating to the side but I can honestly say it didn't bother me one little bit. If anything it made me feel more protective of him. I wanted to be his mum and help him; it only looked like a squint, one that could be corrected fairly easily. We still hadn't heard about the red reflex at that stage, whether or not it was present. We would find out in due course. After our visit we said our goodbyes and left to go home.

That first evening back I felt so many emotions, too many things going through my mind. It didn't feel real. We had just met our children and we were back home as if nothing had happened. I just wanted to get these introductions finished quickly so we could start our new life together. I felt like the two weeks of introductions were going to be a long two weeks. But I was prepared; I knew that eventually we would get through it and be able to bring our two beautiful children home

Day Two

Day two was spent with Sophie. We went to her foster home and spent four lovely hours with her. While we were there, Wendy filled us in on what we needed to know about Sophie. What foods she liked and didn't like, her bedtime routine, her bath time routine etc. It was lovely to spend time with Sophie, for her to see us and get used to us. It still felt a bit strange and awkward being in someone else's home, but we had to do that, mainly for Sophie's sake. It gave her time to get used to us. She was so great, she just completely trusted us, she was happy to be with us. She didn't seem at all confused by the situation. After seeing Sophie, we went home. We didn't see Kallum that day and as strange as it seems so early on, we missed him. I was looking forward to seeing him again.

Day Three

We spent the morning with Kallum. We arrived as he woke from his morning nap and spent time with him during his feed (which went a lot better this time). Katie was very helpful. She went through Kallum's routine, she showed us how to sterilise the bottles, went through when his naps were and how much milk he has. She showed us how to change his nappy, which toys he liked to play with. She was very informative and if it wasn't for her we probably would have found it all a lot harder. It was quite a lot of information but she wrote a lot of it down for us to read later. Kallum was a joy to be with. He was such a lovely baby. I was looking forward to the time when the introductions would be with them both together.

Later that same day we went to see Sophie. We went at three o clock and stayed until after she went to bed. This was a special time because we met the rest of her family. We met her (and Kallum's) half brother and sister. The situation was difficult for them because they were losing Sophie. I think they needed to meet us to see who Sophie was going to be living with. They were amazing kids. It was lovely to meet them and spend the evening with them.

Day Four

On day four we met Katie at the hospital because Kallum had an eye appointment. I was happy to be able to go to the appointment because it meant we could learn more about the problem with his eye and see if the red reflex was present.

It was a good session. The doctor explained that Kallum had a squint in his left eye, and that it might improve over time or he might need some corrective surgery when he was older. She reassured us that it was fairly common. I asked about the red reflex and she said that she could see both. She had no concerns about his vision. That was a great result for us.

After the eye appointment we went back to Katie's house to wait for Wendy who was bringing Sophie so the children could spend time together with us. It was lovely to be together, all four of us, and for Sophie to spend time with Kallum. We had a great time with them, mainly playing.

Wendy mentioned while she was there that Sophie's half-brother was finding it hard. Because he was older than Sophie, he expected to be adopted first and he hadn't been sleeping very well and asked Wendy questions about it all. It was heart-breaking, it really was. It's very difficult

to hear because on one hand I felt guilty, we were taking

Sophie away from him, but on the other had I was excited

about adopting her. After meeting them both, it felt more

real. It just really brings home how complicated things are,

and how much these innocent children are affected by it

all. It made me feel incredibly sad. I can't remember what

day it was but I remember coming home after one visit

and just wanting to ring my mum. It sounds a bit odd, but

I just felt so overwhelmed by the enormity of everything, I

just felt I wanted to speak to mum; I wanted to see her and

tell her all about it. It would have been a comfort to me.

We were told not to involve our families during

introductions because it would be too much for the

children. It was all very intense.

Day Five

This was the first day the children were coming to our house with their Foster Carers; Sophie was arriving first and then Kallum. This was probably the hardest session so far. We were getting to know the children more and we really wanted time to be with them, just us. It was exhausting to keep having sessions with people in the room or house with us. It was an unnatural environment; we couldn't completely be ourselves because we were aware other people were there.

On this occasion we had Sophie with Wendy, Wendy's daughter and a family friend, we had Katie with Kallum, and of course Stacey and myself. That was quite a house full. It felt like it had changed from us trying to get to know the children, to a bit of a social gathering. We hadn't met Wendy's daughter or her friend so it was a bit awkward spending time with them as well as trying to spend time with Sophie and Kallum. Instead of Stacey or me holding Kallum and getting to know him more, he was getting passed around everyone. We just had to stand back and watch. We had been told by the Social Workers we weren't allowed our families involved in the introductions because it would be too confusing for the children. It didn't seem fair. At one point I came into the living room to find Wendy's daughter in floods of tears being comforted by Katie because she was going to miss Sophie. I was struggling with this situation anyway, with the guilt about Sophie's sibling and the awkwardness of the introductions. I felt uncomfortable and awkward having a crying woman in my living room while I was trying to bond with my children. I felt not only was it unfair on us but also on Sophie; it wasn't the time or the place. I felt a lot of pressure. It was with relief that we said goodbye to them all at the end of the session.

That evening we went to Katie's house to watch Kallum's bedtime routine. I have to say that session was one of the best. It was such a contrast to the morning session. It was just Katie, her teenage son, Nathaniel (who cooked us a lovely meal), Kallum, Stacey and I. It was a quiet chilled out evening. Stacey and I bathed Kallum which was lovely. He absolutely loved having his bath. Katie gave us space to do be with him which helped us bond more. I went from feeling overwhelmed and frustrated in the morning to feeling completely at peace with everything in the evening. I felt quite emotional; I just wanted to have Kallum with me all the time. It was a great way to end the day and it renewed my excitement for the placement day. All I wanted was to have some time with the children on our own. I knew we were getting closer.

Day Six

I was very excited about today because we were finally about to spend time with Kallum on our own. We picked him up in the morning and took him to our house for a couple of hours. It was fantastic. At last we could actually be ourselves with each other; we could start to feel what it would be like to have our children home with us. Even though it was just a few hours, it was a lovely time. In the evening we went to see Sophie and watched her bedtime routine. It was nice again to spend time with the family; however the bedtime routine didn't quite go according to plan. I think Sophie knew that we were there for her, so naturally she played up a bit, didn't want to brush her teeth, didn't want to go to bed- she was too excited. To be honest I didn't blame her, it wasn't a natural environment. We had to give up in the end and leave while Sophie was still up and Wendy would put her to bed when we had left.

Day Seven

We had scheduled a meeting with everyone to review how everything had gone and plan the next few days. The general consensus was that we needed to spend longer days with Sophie and Kallum so they could get used to be with us for longer periods of time together in our home. I was really pleased with this because this is what I had been hoping for, our own time with the children.

Days Eight, Nine and Ten

The next three days were fantastic, we had them both all day long, we had lunch with them, we had dinner with them, we bathed them and got them ready for bed and then we took them back to their Foster Carers. It was so nice to finally have quality time with them. By now we had built relationships with them. Sophie had been amazing with us all along. She was so accepting of us, so pleased to see us all the time. She was very affectionate and wanted lots of cuddles, she was a revelation. At first we found getting both their routines to balance together a bit tricky; Kallum had quite a strict routine so we had to try and stick to that as well as giving Sophie our time. I loved those days, they were by far the best times and it also meant we were getting closer to placement. I was longing for the day when we could bathe them, put pyjamas on and instead of putting them in the car and taking them back to their Foster Carers, we could keep them and put them in their beds in their new home with us.

On one of the evenings we had the foster families over our house so that their half-siblings could see where Sophie and Kallum would be living and could picture Sophie when she moved in. It was a lovely evening; it felt a bit like closure for everyone and was nice to finish it in that way. Sophie and Kallum will be keeping in contact with both their half-siblings twice a year, to keep that relationship going. (That will be the only direct contact they will have with any members of their birth family). At the moment they are both a bit young to understand it all, but in time we will be able to explain it to them.

Day Ten

On day ten we took Sophie and Kallum home slightly earlier so they could have their last evening with their foster families. It was also a time for Stacey and me to have our last evening together before placement. It was a lovely evening, because it gave us some time to reflect on what had been going on, and how we felt about tomorrow – the placement day. Even though we were given advice to go out and enjoy our last night before the children came, I was so tired we ended up having a quiet night in. It felt quite surreal; the thought that tomorrow, our children would be home. At last, after all these years and months of trying to start our family, it had finally arrived. Tomorrow was going to be the first day of the rest of our lives. Our lives as we knew it, were about to change dramatically and I couldn't have been more ready. We were just so excited and eager for tomorrow to come.

Day Eleven - Placement Day

October 19ᵗʰ 2012

Placement day! This is the day that I had been longing for, for so long. We had been through so much to get to this stage. We had gone through a couple of years trying to fall pregnant, had tests to discover why we weren't falling pregnant, several years of trying three heart-breaking unsuccessful IVF procedures. We then had eighteen months of jumping through hoops and getting through the

212

rigorous adoption process. We had finally made it, we had (just about) survived it all, and reached placement day. This was the best day of my life! I couldn't believe we had finally got here. I was going to become a mummy to two wonderful, amazing, beautiful children. This is what I had been dreaming about for so long; it seemed unbelievable that at long last my dreams were going to come true. I will never forget how I felt on that momentous day. Emotions were running high with everyone for different reasons. The Foster Carers naturally were feeling emotional because they were going to miss the children; we were feeling emotional and excited because we were finally having the children. We could feel the emotion of the Foster Carers. It was very difficult for them. The transfer had to be quick for the children's sake. Charlie, Sophie's Social Worker was in charge of the transfers; he would be the one to put the children in the car. We could tell that

Sophie knew something different was happening today; she was upset getting into the car. Her Foster Carers said their goodbyes, and then we went to pick up Kallum.

On the way to Kallum's, Sophie seemed better. She could obviously pick up on the emotions of everyone and was upset, but after a while of being in the car with us she settled down, and seemed pleased to see us. Kallum was too young to understand what was happening. He was put into our car by Katie. Katie naturally was struggling with it all, she had had Kallum since he was born and had been with him through his difficult first few months. She had obviously developed a strong connection with Kallum (as had Sophie's Foster Carers). It was difficult for Katie that day; I gave her a big hug, thanked her for everything she had done for Kallum and all the help she had given us. Then as a family we drove off home to start our new lives together full of hope and expectant anticipation of what

214

was to come. I remember looking back in the car at the young faces of Sophie and Kallum and marvelling at how blessed we were to be adopting two such fantastic children. God had really granted us our double blessing.

It was an amazing day, I felt such relief to finish the introductions and have the children finally at home. That was it, they were ours. We still weren't the legal parents of Sophie and Kallum but they were in our care now and as soon as possible we would be able to apply for the adoption order. It was a special and exciting day, one that we will remember forever.

Chapter Twenty Four

Post Placement

It's difficult to put into words how we felt straight after placement day. That first night/morning was the best feeling ever; just knowing the children were in their beds for the first time. I couldn't help but keep checking on them to make sure they were okay. It didn't feel real. It felt a bit like we were babysitting or looking after them for someone. I couldn't quite grasp that this was it. This was our family.

I was so amazed how well Sophie adapted to us and the situation. She didn't ask any questions, she didn't seem upset at all. Quite the opposite, she was full of excitement. She was amazing. It felt so normal, like she had been with us all along. I remember her waking up that first morning and coming downstairs where I was with Kallum. She just came over for a cuddle and asked for a drink. It felt so natural. Stacey had a couple of weeks left of his paternity leave and we had a great two weeks together as a family before Stacey had to go back to work. Our families met the children and we had our friends come and visit. It was quite a whirlwind actually. There was no sign of this hyperactivity that the Social Workers and Foster Carers mentioned from Sophie. Yes, she had lots of energy like any other two year old had; however she also had moments where she would sit with you on the sofa and read a book, or sit and have a cuddle. She was an extremely affectionate child; she just seemed to crave affection. Sophie just took it all in her stride. She didn't seem fazed by any of it. Kallum, being a baby adapted well as long as we stuck to his routine. It took a while to find our feet and learn his routine without having to check the paper we were given. He was a happy baby and smiled and giggled a lot. I loved it; I loved learning everything about having our gorgeous baby. It really was a dream come true.

When Stacey went back to work it was quite hard going balancing both children's needs on my own. I felt a bit 'in at the deep end.' They both needed different things; even going out down the town with them both was quite an ordeal on my own. I would eventually get to town (which in itself was quite a feat), find a cafe, get seated and then Sophie would say she needed the toilet, so we would all have to get back up and find a toilet that would fit us in if there wasn't a baby change available.

I would tell people I would be somewhere at a certain time but end up being about twenty minutes late due to either Kallum being sick as we walked out the door, or needing a nappy change. These are just typical situations for parents I'm sure, but for me during those first few months it was a steep learning curve. I remember on one occasion, Sophie had stubbed her toe on something and started crying. I picked her up to comfort her and then Kallum decided to start crying so I picked him up on the other side. The more Kallum cried, the more Sophie cried, they both got louder and louder. There I was in my kitchen with a screaming and howling child on each hip, trying to outdo each other! It would have been quite comical to watch I'm sure. I had to be careful to give them equal attention where possible. Sophie was used to being in an environment with older children, so she was the youngest in the house. This time she was the older of the two and for the most part she adapted to that role very well. There were times though where, if I was holding Kallum, she wanted to come and have a cuddle. The other thing I noticed is that she would love to play babies. She would be the baby and pretend to cry and her speech would be babbling like a baby. She would want to be comforted the same way you comfort a baby; she wanted to play with baby toys. I don't know if that was because she thought if she acted that way she would get more attention or she was just regressing like they told us about in the adoption classes. If children miss out on a certain time in their lives, at some point they would regress back to that time at an older age. Sophie was put into Foster Care when she was 11 months old, so she wouldn't have had much attention when she was a small baby.

Another area of concern reported by the Foster Carer was that she had no stranger danger. While it was a lovely part of her personality to give cuddles to people and be affectionate, she would do it to everyone. Her Foster

Carer was of an opinion that by then she should have some stranger danger.

When you adopt a child, it is difficult to know whether any unusual behaviours are due to them being a looked after child or just part of their personality and normal for their age. After a while of observing different things and wondering about this and about that from what we had been told by different professionals, I decided to just let it be. Sophie was who she was and whatever the reason for any type of behaviours; it didn't make any difference to us. Sophie was an absolutely delightful and wonderful child and I couldn't believe we were fortunate enough to be her mummy and daddy.

I decided not to go out to any groups to start with because we needed to give the children stability, to let them feel comfortable in our house before taking them to other places and meeting more people. We had a lovely couple of months getting to know each other and learning their personalities. We also had a lot of appointments to keep up with, meeting with the children's Social Workers, registering with GP, Health Visitors, looking into nurseries for Sophie and Kallum's eye appointments. As well as attending the Looked After Child reviews.

I have to say though, by the time January came, I was ready to get out there. I was starting to feel a bit isolated; I needed to meet other mums. I wanted to see where all the baby and toddler groups were, to enjoy the fun side of being a mum.

After placement, you have ten weeks of having shared parental responsibility with the Social Workers. This means for certain things, you need to get the consent off the children's Social Workers, things like medical treatment, dental treatment, if you're staying somewhere else overnight. It sounds a bit of a pain having to keep asking for consent for these things, but in reality it hardly ever came up for us. The only time we requested consent was when we went away to Birmingham which is where Stacey's family are from and we went up there quite a lot. There were never any issues about it. At the end of those ten weeks if everything had gone well, we would then be able to apply for the legal adoption order. That could then take a few months to go through.

During those ten weeks we had visits from the children's Social Worker, Charlie and Alicia, and Jodie, to check how everything was going. The visits started off fairly regularly but then they got less and less. Throughout the whole process, Charlie and Jodie were really positive towards us and supported us whole heartedly; fighting our corner when we needed it. The children adapted very well and it was almost a case of looking for something wrong to tell them. There really were no problems. We were blessed to have them so young so they were able to adapt very quickly.

The ten weeks flew by. We had to have some meetings with the looked after child (LAC) team, to go over how everything had been going and they were fine. Again, no issues to raise. We filled out all the paperwork required to apply for the legal adoption order and on the 26th June 2013 we heard that the order had been granted. That was the official date where everything became legal we had full parental responsibility of Sophie and Kallum. It was a fantastic day because that meant there was nothing anyone could do to take those children away. We were their mum and dad. We had already felt that way ever since they came to live with us, but it was still great to have it officially granted.

Finally, the next date we were waiting for was the celebration hearing. This was the final hearing. It was our chance to celebrate everything that had happened, to have our families with us to join in the celebrations. We all dressed up and went to court to meet with the judge. He thanked us for adopting the children and shook our hands. We had photographs taken with the judge and our families. The children both got a teddy bear to take home with them. Finally we were given an adoption certificate with a family photo on. It was over fairly quickly, but it was nice to take some time out with both families to celebrate what had been the most amazing journey for us.

Chapter Twenty Five

Becoming a Forever Mummy

I obviously can't compare the feelings of being a mum after giving birth to a child to becoming a forever mum, but I can say that from the very first moment I met my children I loved them. I don't believe in love at first sight. I believe you have to get know someone first before saying you love them, but Sophie and Kallum are the exceptions. I knew I loved them the moment I saw them and knew there would be no going back.

I have loved every minute of being their mummy. It hasn't always been easy but I wasn't expecting it to be (especially with two children at once). It has been a joy getting to know them and being part of a wonderful family.

Going through the adoption process, there was always that feeling of having to be good enough, of having to live up to a certain standard. To be the person you think they want you to be, to be the perfect parents. We had to jump through a lot of hoops, not daring to question any of the decisions they had made in case it went against us, and we had to have approval from a lot of different people.

Some of those feelings stayed with me when I first became a mum. I felt like I had to be the best mum in the world because people had said we were approved to adopt. It was almost like we had to prove them right. We had to show how amazing we were, especially as we adopted two. I couldn't show people if I had moments where I felt I couldn't cope. There were times where I felt I had no idea what I was doing, but I would just have a bit of a guess and hope I was doing okay. I felt a bit like I was under scrutiny from people when they found out I had adopted.

I would second guess a lot of things I was doing. Was it

the right thing to do? Should I be doing something else? I

remember one incident where I was in the park and

Sophie needed a wee. There were public toilets there but

I didn't have the right coin so I couldn't use it. Instead, I

decided to let her do a wee in the trees in the park. I

thought to myself that I'd better not let anyone see me

doing this because they may not approve. I ended up

walking with both children as far away as possible in case

anyone could see us and show disapproval to us. We

came back to the park and carried on playing. A few

moments later another mum in the park had a little

daughter who also needed the toilet. She just grabbed her

hand, bent her down by the edge of the park in full view of

everyone, the little girl did the deed and then carried on

playing in the park. The mum just sat down with her

friend and carried on chatting. She made it look such a

natural thing, didn't need to give it a thought. With me I had to think about what was best, what was the right decision, what would people think, etc?

Another time I took Sophie to a ballet show, it was the first show or event we had been involved in. We had paperwork from the ballet school with guidelines about what to take and what not to take. It said not to take chocolate, crisps etc. I packed up the healthiest food bags just in case anyone was checking up on what food we had. I didn't want to run the risk of giving her something unhealthy in case one of the other mums saw and disapproved and wondered how on earth I got approved for adoption (dramatic I know). As it turned out half the mums brought bags of chocolate and crisps for their little girls and no one batted an eyelid. Poor Sophie had to make do with sandwiches, yoghurt and oat & fruit biscuits!

I felt like this for a while. I had that feeling of being put on a pedestal and having to be the best parent in the world. I was very conscious of being an adopted mum rather than a birth mum; it was almost as if I felt pressure to be even better to prove my worth, to prove I was good enough. It was difficult to shake off those feelings of needing to prove ourselves like we had to for so long during the adoption process.

It was exhausting. Trying to second guess everything, trying to make sure I was doing the right thing in other people's eyes as well as my own. In the end I realised I wasn't wondering if I was doing the right thing for the children's sake, it was for other people's approval. I came to the point where I thought I can't keep doing this. I have to be who I am and make the decisions on my own instinct and not keep worrying what other people thought. Nobody was going to take the kids away because I let them eat a milky way or do a wee within eyesight of someone else. I had to have confidence in my own decisions, in my own instincts as a mum. I would make some mistakes I'm sure but I couldn't carry on like this. Once I had made that decision, it was like a weight had lifted off. All I cared about then was what Stacey and I felt about things, what we felt was the best decisions, no matter what anyone else thought. The mums I have met since adopting the children have been the most wonderful people. I have been open about adopting Sophie and Kallum to them and it has been a pleasure getting to know them and sharing stories about our children. The pressure I was feeling was entirely of my own making as a result of a long and arduous process.

I don't worry about any of that kind of thing anymore. (There's plenty of other stuff to worry about!) I just try to be the best mum for Sophie and Kallum because that is what they deserve.

Becoming a mum has taken me on a very long and unexpected journey. As a woman who had her heart set on becoming a mum, it was very difficult for me to come to terms with the fact that I may never have my own natural children. For a long time I wouldn't accept it and kept thinking that it was going to happen for me, wasn't sure how, either naturally or IVF but I was sure it was going to happen. I wasn't ready to think about the alternative.

However, there came a time in my life where I had to seriously think that this may never happen for me. It wasn't an overnight realisation; it was just something that I had to come to terms with. It was something I had to consider. My faith in God gave me the ability to accept this possibility. I really believe that God has been in control of everything in my life. He wouldn't take me through anything that I couldn't handle and I knew that however our journey was going to end, God had the best plans for us, and I had to trust him. That wasn't always easy; many tears have been shed during the low times but it was my trust and faith in God that really made me able to get through it. I don't know why we have certain things happen in our lives, or why God takes us down paths that we find hard, nor why we have to wait a long time to have our dreams fulfilled. What I do believe though, is that through the storms, through the difficulties in life, through the heartaches, God is in control of everything. It is a choice I had to make, to trust in God, to put my life in his hands and to live my life that way. It is because of the difficult times that I can appreciate and celebrate the wonderful times. I could write about so many positives that have come out of the journey we have gone on and

233

that is not including actually adopting two amazing children. If you are going through a difficult time and you can't see an end to it, and, like us, you may have been waiting for years, I would just advise you to hold on, keep the faith and just trust. The best is definitely yet to come.

When the children were placed with us, I felt that we had been given two very precious gifts and we had the honour and privilege to look after these gifts and to nurture them and provide love and stability within set boundaries to help them grow and flourish.

It was hard work and I'm sure there will be a lot more work and challenges ahead of us as they get older but it has been the best thing we could have done. I can honestly say if I had the choice I wouldn't change a thing. I'm so pleased we have gone through this journey of adoption; that this has been our path. It has been enlightening, overwhelming, emotional, nerve racking, exciting and any other emotions you can think of. I have a fantastic husband who has gone through it all with me and who is my everything. I couldn't have done it without him. Stacey is the most amazing person, someone who I trust and love so completely. He has come into his own as a Father, and it is a joy watching him with Sophie and Kallum. It is so wonderful that he is now the Father he has wanted to be for so long. I feel like the most blessed person in the world to have such an amazing family and I can't wait for the rest of our life together building memories.

Right from the moment they were born, Sophie and Kallum have had very difficult struggles. Their little new-born bodies had been damaged through no fault of their own and they have had to fight to both survive and become strong, and for the attention that they should have received (but sadly didn't). Now that Stacey and I have adopted them, they no longer have to fight anymore; we'll

be fighting for them!

Epilogue

When first looking into adoption, the process itself can seem immense, and I'm sure the mere thought of going through it has put many people off enduring it. It can seem a massive undertaking. It definitely is something you can't enter into lightly. It is hard work and at times frustrating. You do have to be very open about everything in your life, nothing can be hidden. In my opinion there are elements of the process that need a lot of looking at and reviewing. It needs to be made more accessible to people and less time consuming and daunting. I understand that there are plans to reduce the PAR stage from eight months to six months and streamlining other parts of the assessment process. This would be a great development.

Despite the long adoption process, my advice to anyone who is thinking about adopting, or maybe you have just started on your journey, is that it is the best thing you will ever accomplish in your life. It is the most rewarding and incredible experience you will go through. Don't look too far ahead in the journey because it will seem very overwhelming. Take it a step at a time and you will get there. There are so many children who need adopting and so many people needed to go through the adoption process. All these children need is for someone to give them a chance; someone to give them the love and stability that they deserve. It's heart-breaking to see how many children there are that need to be adopted. If you have a spare bedroom and love in your heart, please go for it; it is such a privilege to be a part of these children's lives and make a difference to them. You won't regret it.

It took us two years from attending the adoption information evening (June 2011) to having the adoption order granted (June 2013). It was a long process with many up and downs. It is not for the faint hearted, but I truly believe that adopting our children has been the most rewarding experience. Every situation is different and I know our experience was quite a positive and straightforward one. We don't know what the future holds for us as a family, but we are very excited to find out. Adopting my two beautiful children has fulfilled me as a woman. There is no better feeling than tucking my little girl up in bed at night and reading her a story. There is nothing more special than carrying my sleeping baby from the car to his bed, knowing he has complete trust in me. I can't begin to explain the joy they have brought to my life, how much I love them, it feels as though they have always been with us.

I know there are uncertainties about the future but we will face the challenges head on and take it a day at a time. We will enjoy the happy times, cherish the special times and grow together as a family. I thank God every day for bringing Sophie and Kallum into our lives.

I hope you have enjoyed reading my story as much as I have enjoyed writing it.

Lightning Source UK Ltd.
Milton Keynes UK
UKOW06f1455130916

282876UK00020B/327/P